*MOTHERING
YOUR
NURSING
TODDLER*

Painting by Victoria Runge from a photograph of the tomb of Philip V of Spain (1683–1746) and his wife; located in La Granja palace in the mountains near Madrid.

Mothering Your Nursing Toddler

NORMA JANE BUMGARNER

LA LECHE LEAGUE INTERNATIONAL, INC.
FRANKLIN PARK, ILLINOIS

First Edition, July 1980
Revised Edition, December 1982
Second Printing, May 1986

© *1980 by Norma Jane Bumgarner*
© *1982 La Leche League International, Inc.*

All Rights Reserved

Printed in the United States of America

86 87 88 89   9 8 7 6 5 4 3 2

Book and cover design by Lucy Lesiak
Cartoons drawn by Joan McCartney
Cover photo by John T. Franklin, III
Back cover photo © Richard Ebbitt

Library of Congress Catalog Card Number 82-084383
ISBN 0-912500-12-3

Probably none of the children in MOTHERING YOUR NURSING TODDLER are still nursing today. A few are now young parents striving to do their best with their own youngsters. Most of them are students in primary and secondary schools all around the world. To these children—some 1000 or so—this book is dedicated. For without their stories, shared with me by their mothers, this book would not have been possible.

CONTENTS

"Primum non nocere," (first, do no harm) is a well-known medical precept, eminently applicable to the question of how to mother or when to wean. It made a tremendous difference to your two-week-old baby whether you weaned or kept nursing. No question about it. The facts were there, the votes were in and counted. You wean, baby loses. So, despite sore nipples and sleepless nights, you decided to stay on the winning team and keep nursing.

At three months and at six months it was still pretty cut and dried. By a year, though, the pressures and the eyebrows began to go up. "Still nursing?" But you were hooked, (or unhooked, as the case may be) and actually glad your about-to-be toddler still needed you for that special something.

Now he's eighteen months, or maybe two, and you've settled in to being "just a mother." It's not a bad job after all. Your hours are flexible, and you can come and go as you please, provided you take the boss along. And who could ask for a nicer boss than that smiling, chubby little fellow who tags along with you wherever you go? He's such fun to be with. (Even your husband doesn't mind.) So you smile benignly on the doubters.

However, every silver lining has its cloud, and you're beginning to find out that mothering no longer includes giving in to your little one's every desire. You realize that the customer isn't always right anymore, and that you may have to work hard to convince him of that. What he wants and what he needs are no longer necessarily the same. He really doesn't need to run out into traffic, or take apart the morning paper, no matter how much he wants to. All you have to do is ask yourself, "Is it good for him? Bad for him? Does it matter at all?" Most of the time the answer is obvious. So, with infinite patience, cheerfulness, and lots of love and kisses, you set about showing him that, no kidding, there are limits to what he may do.

Nursing needs change, too. People may tell you that your two- or three-year-old doesn't need to nurse anymore. Maybe they're right. On the other hand, maybe they're wrong. It depends on your child. You know him better than they do. Also you know your circumstances better. Again, ask yourself, "Will it be bad for him?" (Will nursing spoil him, keep him a baby, dependent on mommy until he goes to college?) No, it won't hurt him to nurse. He enjoys it, maybe even really needs it, and with lots of "other-mothering" will shortly move on to the next stage of life better equipped to meet the challenges waiting to confront him.

On the other hand, must you nurse this busy little runabout every time he asks for it? Not necessarily. Perhaps your little fellow has just been trying to tell you that he wants more mothering, not just more breast. His real need is for you. Listen to him; look at him; have fun with him. Give him your time. That's quality mothering when your child is small. Turn down the job offers, turn off the soaps. Hang up the phone. Did you know that when you're on the phone you're gone from the neck up? Some kids draw on the walls, or flour the floors. Some just ask to nurse. Maybe the breast is their only reassurance that you still notice them at all. Don't give up nursing too soon. But take care that it is not your child's only link to a too-busy mother. Add more of yourself to your relationship with him and you'll probably find him wanting less of the breast. Talk to other mothers who have gone this route and read MOTHERING YOUR NURSING TODDLER.

You will come away with a better understanding of your own needs as well as those of your child. Your needs are important, but first you must sort them out. Mothers need to learn to sacrifice. They need to learn patience, kindness, and thoughtfulness. Mothers need, above all, a sense of humor to help them through these busy, crazy years. It is tempting to take the short view and make a decision on the basis of our immediate needs (comforts?) when we would be better advised to make a few more sacrifices and put our child's happiness ahead of our own for a little while longer. Later on we'll find out that in doing so we have taken care of some very real needs of our own as well.

Norma Jane has supplied us with excellent guidelines to help us sort out our questions. As one who has nursed her own children, she speaks from first-hand experience. Having talked with many other mothers as well, she reflects a variety of experiences and reactions.

The author explains why some children nurse past infancy, (and why their mothers let them). She tells us how some mothers have answered the curious, handled the pressures, and been good wives to their husbands during these sometimes frustrating, but always fascinating years. She tells us about love and limits at two, three, and four. (Have you ever heard of the "Spicy Burrito Method" of weaning?)

There are no absolutes when it comes to the question of when the post-toddler should wean, so don't look for them here. You have to supply your own answers. I believe Norma Jane has written the nursing mother's "cope" book, of inestimable value to all those who want to gain new insights into life with their little ones.

"There are joys as well as difficulties in every part of parenting," she says. "The nursing years are not the only, or even necessarily the best, of our lives with our children. . . . Good mothering is an investment, not a sacrifice."

I can guarantee that after reading this book you'll find life with your preschooler much easier and lots more fun.

Mary White

Mary White
La Leche League International
Board of Directors
Founding Mother

ACKNOWLEDGMENTS

It seems a lifetime ago—and a lot does happen in seven years—when the idea for this book emerged in long conversations with Judy Greenwood and Elizabeth Hormann. These good friends gave me the confidence to undertake writing for parents of nursing toddlers—certainly the most ambitious project I have ever undertaken.

Pat Hudson deserves a special thank you here. How often, Pat, you will see your ideas reflected or amplified in these pages. For so much of my thinking about mothering grew out of conversations and correspondence with you.

I could never have succeeded without the patience of my husband and children. Nor would I have had much of interest to say without the lessons we learned in rearing our children through their preschool years.

I am grateful to Sue Forrester, my long-time friend and colleague in La Leche League, for sharing her experience with me, for fulfilling some of my commitments when I was too involved in writing to do other things I had promised, and especially for reading and commenting thoughtfully on the manuscript when it was still in unbearably rough form.

I owe special thanks to Dr. Gregory White of La Leche League's Professional Advisory Board, and to his wife, Mary White, one of the founding mothers of La Leche League, for their careful reading of the manuscript and their many helpful comments and suggestions.

The artist, so talented and special to me, who did the beautiful painting for the frontispiece is my mother, working from a photograph by my colleague and friend, Mari Carmen Mariscal.

I am grateful to Niles Newton, PhD, for information on nursing while pregnant, material from a study she did along with Marilyn Theotokatos. Karen Fitzgerald kindly shared some of her expertise as a nutritionist. Linda Kay Griffin did an excellent job proofreading the final typescript. Mary Ann Kerwin and the La Leche League International Book List Committee, including Alice Bicknell, were most helpful and encouraging. Judy Torgus provided invaluable assistance with many last-minute details.

My thanks go also to Harper and Row, Publishers, Inc., for their permission to quote Gussie's story from Betty Smith's *A Tree Grows in Brooklyn,* and to John Bowlby, The Tavistock Institute of Human Relations, London, and Basic Books, Inc., New York, for permission to quote excerpts from *Attachment.*

AN INVESTMENT, NOT A SACRIFICE

When I first saw a walking child nurse, I was horrified—horrified at the kind of sacrifices the mother must be making for her child, horrified at what I saw as the obscenity of it, and horrified at the lack of good parental management that had let this thing go on so long. As I got to know that mother and child better, though, my view changed. I did not see her making any unneeded sacrifices; she seemed to enjoy nursing. Nor was there lack of parental management when it was called for; both parents were actively teaching their son how to care for himself and how to show respect for the rights and property of others. As time went on I saw that their nursing was not some weird perversion either; nursing was clearly a warm and tender part of their life together, one of many ways these two people loved and enjoyed each other. So impressed was I with the kind of relationship they had and what she was able to tell me about extended nursing that when my next child was born, I did not wean her. I let weaning come in its own time. Through example and experience I was happily able to learn that weaning does not have to be imposed upon a child and that nursing can—and should—continue as long as mother and child want it to.

DOWN WITH MARTYRDOM

For almost half a century women have been stirring, rising, and at last revolting against needless sacrifices that have long been expected of women, especially in the name of children, including oftentimes what many saw as the "sacrifice" of nursing at all, and especially nursing "forever." This revolution has been partially on target, for in human relationships excessive sacrifice tends to be a deadly trap. Mothers who have thought that their role was to do everything for everybody all the time, never asking anything for themselves, have given motherhood a terrible reputation. The tragic picture of the guilt-ridden son weeping over the grave of his mother, who has spent her youth and beauty, if not her very life on him, is sadly a romantic ideal in our culture that shows up repeatedly in our literature and art. Romantic or not, however, more and more women have come to see this picture as one they want to stay out of if at all possible. After all, everyone in it is—or was—unhappy.

In fleeing this picture, however, many have gone too far. Some mothers have so recoiled from the idea that the only value their lives had was in the "success" of other family members that they have left the family and tried to start a new life alone or with other single women. In great numbers other women have seemed to withdraw from the care of their children without leaving home, and usually without even intending to withdraw, choosing to bottle feed, forcing infants and young children to sleep all night and alone, and forcing toilet training as early as possible. Care for young children by someone besides mother has come to be seen as a right which mothers have rather than as an option to benefit those children who enjoy a world with more people in it. We have even allowed a kind of economy to develop in which in some families both parents have to leave their children in order to earn enough to feed them.

The problem mothers have faced over the years of changing the picture is figuring out what sacrifices are necessary and are, therefore, not sacrifices at all but investments. In devaluing sacrifice per se as the mark of a "good mother," we must try to define the many things that mothers in the past were feeling obligated to do that they should have been seeing as optional. We have become very confused about what we are committed to do for our families by the fact that we have become mothers and what we might want to do for them if we have time and energy left over.

FINDING THE ESSENTIALS

In our efforts to move away from duties of motherhood that have seemed uncomfortable and sometimes quite unfulfilling, we have left bare and sometimes even torn up the foundation of the family, a foundation which had somehow gotten lost under a clutter of roles and obligations for every member of the family. That foundation is human need. As destructive to family life as some of our flight from motherhood has seemed, we have at least been able to learn from it more about what is and what is not indispensable in family life—in our roles as mothers, fathers, sons, and daughters.

The family is a grouping of people which is ideally suited to meeting the kinds of needs that human beings have. Families can provide for their own members better than any other social grouping. The family is not, we are learning at last, a gathering of people around a mother who takes care of them all, or around a father who takes care of them all. Families are groups of people who take care of each other.

Every member of the family, including mother, has certain biological and emotional needs. It is necessary for members of a family to see that all these needs are met for every member of the family, for if someone is lacking any of these essentials, life will be difficult for the whole group.

It is only when the essential needs are being met that we can begin to consider extras like a larger income and interior decoration. It is in our ranking of needs and extras that we have gotten ourselves into trouble. We have turned our backs on our families because of what we have to do to get a new house or car, and to keep those things clean and shiny, and to keep ourselves shaped just so, and to stay in this or that social circle, and so on and on.

No doubt we can manage quite a number of these things while each of us does our part in seeing that everyone at home is faring well. It is the accumulation of so many "essential" things that does us in. When we turn away from a crying child in order to clean a carpet—or to buy a new one—we can be sure that our values are backwards. It should not be surprising how little pleasure there is in the spotless carpet when someone in the house is unhappy. We are learning at last that what we have to do in life is to help each other fulfill our needs. Everything else is extra—fine, but only if we have resources to spare above the human needs around us.

TENDING TO BASICS MAKES LIFE EASIER—NOT HARDER

Making the commitment to help another adult meet his or her needs, as in marriage, may seem frightening, especially when we are very young. Yet such a commitment clearly makes life easier, for it is an agreement to help each other from the very beginning of the marriage relationship—or it should be.

With our children the commitment seems one-sided at first. Babies and young children are totally dependent upon us. The impulse to evade such total responsibility for another is easy to understand, especially the first time we are parents. Yet experience shows that the more we are able to give ourselves to the basic needs of the young child—almost all of which can be satisfied by nursing in the beginning—the easier life is. As one mother said looking back on her first mothering experience, "In retrospect, my attitude then seems so silly. My husband and I spent hours rocking her—at all hours of the day and night—when a few minutes at the breast would have been a great time and effort saver." Yet this struggle against giving ourselves fully to the baby seems to be a part of learning to be parents for so many of us. I know it was for me.

Almost every modern book on the psychology of children discusses the ill effects upon children and their families from premature or harsh weaning, toilet training, and bedtime restrictions. These books are not written in praise of how much easier are the lives of those who have imposed restrictions upon children in order to free adults for other "more important" tasks. These books are written because families are troubled when non-nurturing child care practices have backfired.

Yet it takes time for many of us to learn what one mother in Denmark discovered with her first child: "Laziness was probably the strongest urge that got me to nurse so well and to fulfill my child's needs in his earliest months, and it was also what kept me nursing. It is much easier to put a tired, bored, thirsty, hungry, and demanding eight-month, ten-month, fourteen-month-old child to the breast when you are visiting friends and want to talk. It is much easier to have enough milk so he will be satisfied in the early morning hours when I want to sleep." I am always envious of and impressed by parents who do not have to try avoiding their children's needs for a while before they learn how much simpler and happier life can be when needs are tended to immediately.

Giving freely to the young child is not a sacrifice either, though it may feel like a sacrifice at times. It is, as I have said, an investment. Before your child is grown there will doubtless be days when you in turn are totally dependent upon him (for example, when you come down with that twenty-four-hour "bug"). Your first-rate care for your child when he needs you will give him the resources once he is old enough to do as good a job for you when you need him.

Meeting human needs in our children not only helps them grow into psychologically healthy adults; it also helps each of them to learn how to do their part in the family as a group formed to take care of each other.

BREASTFEEDING IS ONE OF THE BASICS

Breastfeeding does require a great deal of commitment and dedication at times. I do not want to imply that it is always without effort, for it is not. It is often an intense and demanding occupation for about two years—maybe one, maybe three—though nursing may continue at a more relaxed pace for much longer. During the times when the child's nursing is frequent and urgent, it is harder for a mother to see that what she is doing is liberating her. Yet a desire to avoid drudgery is a very good reason to nurse and to nurse as long as the child expresses the need, for to deny intensive mothering to a young child is to risk making family life much more difficult in the present and the future. The ease that nursing brings to coping with tantrums and bedtimes is sufficient in itself to motivate most mothers. Nursing makes the job of mothering easier, not harder.

Of course there are times when providing the care and attention required by small children can be maddening, but to

abandon the task can have results that are even more maddening. It is far safer and more reliably easy to relax into
human biological patterns of child rearing and turn away if
necessary from some inanimate parts of the family's life for a
while. To do so may seem like sacrifice at the time, but the
sacrifice of inanimate things is only temporary. A movie that
you miss this year will be at the drive-in next year. An
unmade bed will look just as nice once you get around to
making it, no matter how long it stays unmade. A neglected
career may be difficult to re-enter, but happily mothers are
fighting to make even that less and less true.

Increasingly we are learning for sure that if we turn away
from our children instead of turning away from things, the
children's unmet needs may grow in them and burden them
and their families in one way or another for years to come. It is
usually easier to do the hard work of mothering—to do it
right, and do it when it needs to be done.

One woman says on this subject, "As for my needs, nursing is the easiest, most pleasant of all the 1000 things a mother
must do for a child, so why begrudge him that?" A non-
sacrificing mother, one who wants to be free to do her own
thing, will probably have the most opportunity possible within her particular family if she helps and encourages other family members to do their own thing too. Her little one's "thing"
for a while will be nursing, using diapers, and needing lots of
care day and night.

HOW WE SEE THE NURSING COUPLE

The way I saw the first nursling who was more than a tiny
infant turns out to be a rather standard reaction in our time
and in the way of thinking we have developed in the Western
world.

Jane Goodall, whose work I admire very much, with all
the sensitivity and regard she has for the nursing relationship
still shows some effects on her thinking of Western culture's
twentieth-century view of the older nursling—especially a
demanding youngster—in her book, *In the Shadow of Man*. She
interprets the behavior of the young chimpanzee, Flint, more
with concern for the wear and tear he makes on his mother's
energy and patience than with regard for Flint's displacement

by a younger sibling and then the subsequent death of that sibling. Having become accustomed to the behavior of youngsters who need to nurse past infancy, the description of Flint's regression to infantile behavior makes me think of a little one who has been weaned before he is ready and is desperate to have his mother back for a while yet, not as Ms. Goodall sees him, as one who was not weaned soon enough or firmly enough.

More than this mild difference in viewpoint, a truly distorted picture of the nursing child has crept into our families and into our literature, like this grotesque account from Betty Smith's *A Tree Grows in Brooklyn:*

> Gussie, a boy of six, was a murky legend in the neighborhood. A tough little hellion, with an over-developed underlip, he had been born like other babies and nursed at his mother's great breasts. But there, all resemblance to any child, living or dead, ceased. His mother tried to wean him when he was nine months old but Gussie wouldn't stand for it. Denied the breast, he refused a bottle, food or water. He lay in his crib and whimpered. His mother, fearful that he would starve, resumed nursing him. He sucked contentedly, refusing all other food, and lived off his mother's milk until he was nearly two years old. The milk stopped then because his mother was with child again. Gussie sulked and bided his time for nine long months. He refused cow's milk in any form or container and took to drinking black coffee.
>
> Little Tilly was born and the mother flowed with milk again. Gussie went into hysterics the first time he saw the baby nursing. He lay on the floor, screaming and banging his head. He wouldn't eat for four days and he refused to go to the toilet. He got haggard and his mother got frightened. She thought it wouldn't do any harm to give him the breast just once. That was her big mistake. He was like a dope fiend getting the stuff after a long period of deprivation. He wouldn't let go.
>
> He took all of his mother's milk from that time on and Little Tilly, a sickly baby, had to go on the bottle.
>
> Gussie was three years old at this time and big for his age. Like other boys, he wore knee pants and heavy shoes with brass toe tips. As soon as he saw his mother unbutton her dress, he ran to her. He stood up while nursing, an elbow on his mother's knee, his feet crossed jauntily and his eyes roving around the room. Standing to nurse was not such a remarkable feat as his mother's breasts were mountainous and practically rested in her lap when released. Gussie was

indeed a fearful sight nursing that way and he looked not unlike a man with his foot on a bar rail, smoking a fat, pale cigar.

Poor Gussie. In this account the very young child comes across, not as a very small person who is not yet ready to give up his babyhood, but as an obscene little man. Nor did Betty Smith create such a harsh picture out of deliberate lack of warmth and kindness toward children, for her writing is filled to overflowing with tenderness and concern for the very young. Rather this description of Gussie's nursing is a remarkably accurate portrayal of our society's image of the nursing child. (For the rest of this story, see Chapter 16.)

No one seems to be able to see how resourceful Gussie is for one so young in his ability to tell his mother what his needs are. Apparently no one is around who knows that with greater peace and less family disruption the mother could have met both Gussie's needs and Tilly's. The tale is tragic, not funny.

The reason that the description of Gussie's behavior seems to be thoroughly obscene is that it is presented in adult terms. Gussie is described as a plotting dope fiend, a man at the bar with a cigar, a monster, a dice-player (these latter, further on in the account)—all these descriptions for someone who is going on four and whose second teeth might not come in straight! Yet when we have never seen a nursing child before, distorted vision like this is understandable: We have only adult references from which to look at him.

Hopefully more experience with older nurslings will give us appropriate, child-oriented frames of reference in which to see the behavior of the nursing child. We will be able to realize the special and wholesome kind of relationship there is between a mother and her suckling child, even if this child is big, even if this child is dressed in "big boy" clothes. Then a nursing child will not look to us like a horrid little man smoking a cigar. Instead we will see the baby still peeping out of those big-boy eyes. And we will see the joy in those eyes that mother is still there ready to care for that baby.

EXCESSIVE MANAGEMENT OF CHILDREN'S LIVES

Somehow part of our distorted view of little children has generated distrust in us toward children and their ability to grow up. More and more we have jumped in and tried to take control over every aspect of their living. We have overwhelmed ourselves with things we must do for our children, and what is so ludicrous about much of this activity and interference with our children's lives is that all our work supposedly makes life easier for us adults. What nonsense!

We make up schedules for feeding babies, watch clocks, and carefully measure what they eat. We thrust spoons and cups into little hands that do not even pattycake very well yet. We monitor their toilet habits, their bedtimes, and the way they treat the statuary and potted plants. We decorate their rooms and fuss constantly over how they are dressed and whether their toes point the right direction. If they are not sleeping all night by six months, we try hard to do something about the "problem." If they aren't toilet trained by one and a half or two, what a worry. And a year-old child who is not weaned, or certainly well on the way toward weaning—oh, dear, we must do something and fast!

We clean our children's rooms, keep up with their clothing, and cook all their meals—sometimes for years. And then when they reach adolescence and need us again to be perceptive and thoughtful and loving, we wonder why we are too worn out to love them through their second time in life of enormous growth.

Our children do not need to have their lives managed or to have someone plan every aspect of their growth. Children do not cling to nursing or diapers or waking at night or even finger the household ornaments in order to trouble or control adults or even out of bad habits. They do these things because of needs and drives inside themselves. It is ever so much more wholesome for the growing child and easier for the whole family—believe it or not—especially for mother, just to forget managing infantile behaviors.

It is healthy, constructive, and ever so much more relaxing to go through life with your young child not dreading battles over night wakings, or worrying about when your child will eat next or need to use the bathroom next.

FINDING THE BABY AMONG THE TEDDY BEARS

Of course many mothers love some of the time-consuming tasks that mothers can take on, such as providing elaborate nursery decorations. These niceties are the right of any mother who has time and resources to spend on them. But they are for the mother, and no one should feel duty bound to provide a baby with such extras as traditional nursery surroundings. The infant does not care much about them. Most young children prefer their parents' bed to the most beautiful nursery in the world anyway. By the time a child is interested in how his room is decorated, he is old enough to do it himself—and without much advice (he would call it "bossing around") from mother.

The same is true for clothing. The young child enjoys comfort and variety, and hand-me-downs are often best in this regard. By the time he cares how they look, he will want to choose his own. We parents do enjoy seeing our children nicely dressed, so we should feel free to put pretty clothes on our little ones as long as doing so does not interfere with something important and as long as they are happy with our choices. But again we must know that we are dressing them for our own sakes. Not to put them into pretty clothes while they are indifferent to what they are wearing deprives them of nothing.

THE REAL GOAL FOR PARENTS—SELF-SUFFICIENCY

Too often mothers, even as the children get older, keep the essential family business of preparing meals, house cleaning, and keeping clothes clean and sorted to themselves—maybe as a realm preserved only for mothers so that she is indispensable to the family—or maybe as a woman's duty to her family, duties with which she would never dare ask for help. By keeping any task to herself, however, a mother is doing her family no favor. She is depriving every member of her family of the security of knowing that, if necessary, he or she can survive.

A primary job in parenting is to teach each child the necessary skills to take care of himself. Every daughter and every son should be able to tend the house, prepare food, wash and mend clothing, go to the store, pump gasoline, or change a tire. It is not our job as parents simply to take care of our children, but to help them learn how to take care of themselves.

So, rather than fretting over toilet training or weaning in the toddler years—these are things which will take care of themselves—it is more constructive to help children learn to do the things they want and need to do. This will likely include helping the child master the mysteries of slicing cheese or pouring milk, buttoning coats, and letting the dog out. By school age, most children should have learned to sort laundry and operate the washing machine. Soon they can prepare a hot meal from cans or simple recipes.

It should not be the parents' objective to manage children's lives, nor to be their caretakers. Nothing is more pitiful than to have a whole family in panic because a parent is down with the flu. All of us—mothers, fathers, and children—need to learn everything we can so that we can cope with every circumstance and take care of each other. Second-graders make delicious pancakes, and preschoolers can bring great cheese and apples to a mommy who is under the weather. Daddies sew on buttons just fine. Mommies can put jumper cables on dead batteries. And big brothers can build a fire in the fireplace or wash and dry synthetics without setting in wrinkles.

There is nobody in the family who can be sure of never being called upon to do someone else's job. There is no one who is not terrified of being left helpless if an irreplaceable caretaker becomes ill or dies. In love and kindness to ourselves and to our families we should spend less time—or better yet—no time on managing nursing and sleeping and toileting. We should not try to monitor every bite our children eat, every item of clothing they wear, or exactly how they maintain their rooms. Rather we should embark upon a long-range plan in rearing our children which includes spending no more time than we need doing for other family members what they have been able to learn to do for themselves. (Note the phrase "than we need" in the previous sentence—family business does proceed more efficiently when there is a comfortable division of labor.)

We should think in terms of helping our children learn to care for themselves when they must, and to do even parents' jobs when need be—or sometimes even just for fun. The more people know how to do, the more confidently they can live—and the easier life is for everyone, including mother. As a bonus, as if one were needed beyond the joy of self-confidence that we can give our families, when we mothers are not burdened by long lists of tasks we must do for our children for as long as they live with us, then the times of their lives when they need a lot from us will seem ever so much less overwhelming. The nursing years, for instance, are not an ongoing pattern of unending service from mother to child. Soon, perhaps even before nursing is completely ended, mother and child will clearly be doing for each other.

We waste precious time and energy—time and energy we could use for our many other and no doubt more pleasant ambitions—in trying to avoid the enormous investment of ourselves that a very young child needs. We hope we can avoid having to commit ourselves so fully, and we fear that the demands of the young child will go on forever. Yet it is not so. It is an economical move in terms of our own personal resources, even a laudably selfish move, to give ourselves fully to the infant and young child. For as Dr. Lee Salk, well-known writer and lecturer in child psychology, points out, a child's needs for intensive parenting, like needs for food, go away once they are satisfied and remain when they are not.

There is no form of parental management which will teach a young child not to hunger for great helpings of attention. Rather than wasting effort, to say nothing of peace and potentially happy times, in trying to teach a young child to get along with less of her parents' days and nights, it is far wiser to give that time freely, and to make good use of it for teaching really valuable and lasting lessons—like how to love, how to play, and where to find the peanut butter.

PART I

Nursing Your Toddler —Why?

CHAPTER 1

Why Children Nurse into Toddlerhood

SUCKING—A TOOL FOR GROWING

It may seem strange at first that a child who sits at the family table at mealtimes and is into the refrigerator many times in between would also ask his mother for nursing several times a day—and night.

Yet anyone who looks lovingly at a child at the breast can see that eating is only a part of nursing. After a minute or two of nursing, the entire little body relaxes with contentment and pleasure. A child who is hurt begins to feel better. A child who has become overexcited calms down. One mother says of her nursing child, "She'll come up to me whining and refusing to talk. We'll sit and nurse; and then she'll hop down and act like a big person again, having total control."

When we think about it, Betty Smith's comparison of the nursing child to a dope fiend is not entirely off the mark. Nursing for the child is a kind of "fix," but an entirely healthy one. It is not addictive, but just the opposite. It is no wonder that some families call mother's milk "joy juice." Nursing has all the restorative powers of a morning cup of coffee without raising the child's blood pressure. It is as relaxing as an evening cocktail, with no bleary aftereffects.

Sucking is a necessary leveler for rapidly growing little people—so much so that most children who do not nurse seek an alternative—bottle, pacifier, thumb, fingers, hair, blanket-corner, etc. . . . They show us through the persistence of such behaviors that young children need the calming and reassuring effects of sucking as much or more than some of us adults need our "pacifiers." For they are so young, so immature, so without experience in this world; and yet they are undergoing enormous growth and changes that are incomprehensible to them.

It is a blessing given to babies and little children that they can be at ease at times through the physical and mental upheaval—greater than adolescence—that races them from the womb into childhood in just a few short years. Children have the ability to be awakened and relaxed, to be soothed and comforted through sucking.

Of such sucking John Bowlby, who has spent so much of his time in psychiatric research studying the attachment (dependency) behavior of young children says:

> In primates, nipple-grasping and sucking have two separate functions, one for nutrition and a second for attachment. Each of these functions is of importance in its own right, and to suppose that nutrition is in some way of primary significance and that attachment is only secondary would be a mistake. In fact, far more time is spent in nonnutritional sucking than in nutritional.

The very best place for this sucking to take place is in mother's arms, at her breast, where it is entirely natural and complete. The simple act of sucking is transformed into the complete act of suckling, which includes not only sucking, but also the special mouth and tongue actions required for milking the breast—and all within the embrace of mother and child.

Suckling plays an enormous role in a child's ability to grow up. Some children, unless their mothers nurse them or help them find substitutes, may never completely overcome the anxieties and confusion they experience through the changes of their early years. Some seek ineffective substitutes, either in behaviors or in objects. Unlike suckling, however, which will cease all by itself once it has done its job, the dependence upon less effective behaviors or upon objects may not go away nearly so easily or reliably.

WHAT NURSING CHILDREN TELL US

As children grow older, some are able to put into words their reasons for nursing. And their reasons are neither manipulative nor evil as some people seem to think. At two and a half, one of my children told me, "I 'nanny' when I feel like a baby."

Often we say that a child nurses only for closeness with mother after the first year or so, not for the milk. In a sense this statement is true, for a child who eats a wide variety of table foods does not require the nourishment of mother's milk. As one father put it, "She's no longer refilling her tanks; she's recharging her batteries!"

In another sense, though, children do nurse for the milk, because they like it. "I'm sure thirsty for your milk inside of you," one three-year-old told his mother. "Delicious!" announced a two-year-old when she had finished nursing. "It's my favorite!" said another, in the manner of a young gourmet offering compliments to the chef. According to one child, mother's milk is "the most delicious milk in the whole world."

Good milk, Partner!

What mother has to offer is so good that little ones often want their dolls and teddy bears to have a share—and sometimes even their playmates, though the playmates invariably decline. One little guy even asked his mother to refuel his new truck! He wanted only the best for his prized possession. Children are quite aware, however, not only of nursing for milk, but also of nursing for comfort, and talk about this "non-nutritive" sucking sometimes, too. One two-year-old offered to nurse her mother who was not feeling well. "It will make you feel better fast, Mommy," she promised. A four-year-old, also thinking about nursing for comfort, modified "Jack and Jill" so that it made more sense to her: "Jack fell down, and broke his crown, and went home for num-num."

An articulate five-year-old had thought the matter of his continued nursing through quite thoroughly. He told his mother:

> I think five-year-olds should be able to nurse if they want to. I think five-year-olds should enjoy nursing. Nursing is like drinking from a bottle except it's more comfortable. It feels very good, and I'm next to Mommy.

Though few children verbalize their thoughts about nursing so completely as this young man, we can be sure that our children do think about it and that their thoughts and motivations are along these lines. When children talk about nursing, they talk about something very warm and special to them. Nursing is their "soul food." They nurse because it tastes good and feels good and helps them to be happy.

CHAPTER 2

Why Mothers Nurse
Their Children
into Toddlerhood

SEEING A NEED

When I ask mothers who have nursed longer than a year why they chose to do so, they usually say, "It just seemed natural," or, "He seemed to need it still." Some mothers, taking their cues from the child rather than the calendar, say, "I never even thought about it."

One mother describes the way she felt about her child's continued nursing: "I knew and felt her need for me and her desire to nurse. I love her, and it would break my own heart to disappoint her and refuse myself to her." If we look past all the social rules and look at the children these rules are supposed to benefit as did this mother, it is not difficult to see the need our children have for continued nursing—their joy in nursing and their distress when it is denied. A simple but compelling reason for continuing to nurse is to please the child. More and more mothers are watching their children and seeing the need that is there.

THE PLEASURE OF CLOSENESS

Nursing is not only for the benefit of the child. Mothers enjoy nursing too. As one mother puts it, "I think I would be

18

crushed if a baby only wanted to nurse a year. This is because I probably enjoy nursing as much as the baby does." No matter how evil some people may make mother's enjoyment sound, a mother's pleasure in nursing is a good thing—one of the many wholesome pleasures available in life.

Being very close to a warm, cuddly child is the advantage mothers like best about extended nursing. "I used to believe," one mother says, "any mother who continued nursing after so many years had unmet needs of her own that nursing was satisfying." But this mother found as her own nursling grew older that those "unmet needs" she was worried about were actually normal, healthy needs that are intended to be met by nursing.

No matter how much effort has gone into the selling of distance between mother and child, distance achieved by mother substitutes like playpens and pacifiers, and by child substitutes like hobbies and pets, mothers it seems cannot be changed. We still are happiest when we can hold our children close.

So precious is the intimacy between mother and child, and unique and irreplaceable in the lives of both mother and child, that it seems everyone who sees the pair would do whatever is in his power to protect that bond. Indeed artists sometimes capture a bit of the warmth of a mother and child in poetry or paint. "I once heard," a mother told me, "that bottle-feeding is like making a close friendship; breastfeeding is like having a love affair—and I truly believe this just from my own experience."

Yet, sadly, and with the cooperation of many families, people who were charged with or took upon themselves the public nurturing of mothers and their children through instructions and advice on child care over the years developed systems that struck at every element in the relationship between mother and child that we so admire.

It is little wonder that many of us are overjoyed to rediscover the closeness we can have with our children. One mother said as she looked back at her nursing time, "The memory of nursing my daughter as a toddler is very pleasant for me. It is hard to pick out one best aspect. I remember the closeness, how comfortable I felt having her always near me. I remember how confident I felt in almost always being able to comfort her and knowing instinctively how to meet her needs whether it involved nursing or not, the beautiful loving feeling I had for her, and which she returned, and the pride I felt at being the mother of this beautiful, bright child."

We may never have even seen this kind of completely natural mother-child relationship in all our growing up. Having discovered how good it feels to be intimately bonded with a baby and young child, more and more of us are learning again to give up this closeness for nothing except the gradual progress of maturation.

Nursing is instrumental in establishing intimacy between mother and child. In the beginning the physical and chemical interactions involved in nursing help the bond to establish properly. Continued nursing helps to maintain it by giving both mother and child an appropriate pattern for intimate behavior.

This loving behavior helps overcome other factors in the child's rapid development which can interfere with closeness. Some children are very shy and tend to withdraw from close interaction with people, even mother. The shy child who is still nursing has a ready-made assertive behavior through nursing that can help him to learn how to get his other needs met, too.

Other children are so active that nursing time is the only quiet, level time in their busy waking hours. Nursing time is especially refreshing for the mother of a little run-about; and mothers of very active toddlers treasure nursing times perhaps more than anyone else. One mother says, "So many of my friends weaned early. They lost those special close moments as their children became more active. My son is just as active and independent, but we can both look forward to our special moments." It is much easier to feel close and loving toward a child in arms than toward one who is on top of the cabinets or dumping the flower pots.

As surprising as it may seem, a small percentage of babies inexplicably form their primary attachment with someone in the family other than mother (Bowlby). In these families the mother's need for her child's attention (How seldom we think of what a mother needs from her child. . . .) could be at risk. One nursing mother wistfully told me, "My little boy has been a daddy's boy from the beginning. At least he comes to me to be nursed!" For her own sake a mother whose child chooses to spend most of his time with daddy or big sister or someone else in the household would be ill-advised to hasten weaning—at least not until the child grows older and becomes interested in more people, including mother.

There are children, too—usually boys, but not always—who are difficult to manage. These little people are going all the time, active and demanding. Responding warmly to the needs that these children show for nursing may be difficult at times because of the negative feelings their behavior naturally tends to generate in us. It is interesting, though, that we usually have these bad feelings about nursing when our children seem demanding in front of other people. At home we can usually cope with our little "wild men" much better.

At the same time that their behavior ruffles our feelings about nursing them, though, the calm of nursing in turn helps to smooth over our annoyances. Mothers who have nursed an unusually active and demanding toddler until he became a reasonably civilized child look back on the experience and realize what an advantage nursing was for them. Without the regular intervals of loving that nursing provided, it would have been more difficult for them to keep the interactions between mother and child more positive than negative.

Mothers too can get into behaviors (usually referred to as "things I have to do") that can prematurely disrupt the mother-child bond. Just as nursing is the only time active toddlers hold still for loving, so nursing is the only time some busy mothers sit still for that same loving—loving which these mothers need as much as less active mothers do.

A TOOL FOR COMFORT

Nursing is not only a pleasure, but also quite a convenience. A major task in mothering is helping your child several times daily to overcome fears or hurts or exhaustion. There are various ways to comfort a crying child—walking, rocking, singing—but none is easier or more efficient than nursing. It has been described as a little bit of magic on your side: Presto, a fussy child is happy again.

It is nothing short of amazing how quickly a bruise or a scrape stops hurting when the first-aid includes nursing. And if it is more than a bruise or a scrape, the fact that nursing does not seem to make the pain go away tells you quickly that you are dealing with a bigger hurt that may need extra attention. Other methods do quiet children, too, but the psychological network of the very young seems to be wired with nursing as the choice channel for feeling better. Though not all children will verbalize it, nursing toddlers no doubt appreciate nursing for comfort as much as did the two-year-old who, having fallen and then nursed, amply rewarded her mother by saying, "Thanks, Mom, for nursing me. 'Bye now, I'll be okay."

Teething is the most recurrent physiological cause for discomfort in little children, and when new teeth are making their gums sore, little ones often ask for a great deal of time at the breast. Many a nursing mother has been pleased to help her child through the discomfort of teething with nursing alone, or perhaps with nursing for soothing and cold celery for biting. Of course we are glad sometimes for the relief that aspirin or anesthetic ointments can bring when gums get really painful. It is gratifying, however, to be able to keep our reliance upon chemical comforters to a minimum through use of a natural analgesic—nursing.

Little people also manage to bump their mouths frequently, especially while they still walk unsteadily, and even very small injuries to the mouth tend to bleed profusely. Toddlers usually hate having pressure and ice applied to their mouths to stop the bleeding. They do like to nurse, however, and most of the time nursing puts enough pressure on the injured mouth tissue to do the job. For the ordinary small mouth injuries that toddlers suffer so frequently nursing is the best first-aid, and usually all that is needed.

Comforting a sleepy child at bedtime and naptime is so easy for families when the little one is nursing. Rarely do nursing families experience the fuss and tension we have come to expect in our culture when a little one needs to go to sleep. Nursing is so effective a tranquilizer for tired children that fathers tease their wives about their "knock-out drops." Few families who have experienced a nursing child's bedtime or naptime will ever want to rear a child any other way.

Mothers also nurse their children to help them overcome upsets, emotional as well as physical. Most mothers, even if they do plan to wean, refrain from doing so during an upheaval such as a family crisis or a move. Nursing is too beneficial to children when their families are upset or in transition to cut it off at a time when the child may especially need it. One mother whose family experienced half a year of illness and loss wrote about nursing her daughter during this difficult time: "Nursing has certainly helped her; it has been like an anchor in a storm. Whatever else has happened, Mummy's milk has always been there."

Nor are the children the only ones who are comforted by nursing when the family is under stress. So many mothers, for example, tell how, instead of weaning when they are facing emotional stress as is often advised, they used nursing as one way to soothe themselves. "When my grandmother died," one mother wrote, "I picked my son up and nursed him." "I have been depressed since Dad died," another said, "and nursing my little daughter has helped." Still another mother overcoming grief wrote that nursing provided "periods of reality in a stress-filled time. It forced me to keep it all together."

The comfort that nursing provides is often mutual, shared by mother and child.

A HEALTH PLUS

The one time when we are most grateful for our ability to help our child by nursing—more than with a bruised knee or sore gums—is when the child is ill. Having a child ill can make us feel more helpless than any other problem in life. To be able to do nothing but sit beside a whimpering, miserable child, watching the clock for the next appointed time for medication, is a wretched business. I do not know who receives the greatest relief from the misery of a child's illness through nursing—mother or child.

Once we have broken away from the image of an ill child tucked neatly away into bed and mother standing dutifully by, we are able to tune in to our own feelings and instincts. The only place for a small child who is ill is in our arms, and we cannot feel any peace within ourselves when he is anywhere else. Children come through illnesses, even serious ones, much less fretfully if they are held, and if they can nurse, so much the better.

Even children who must be hospitalized can usually be held by their parents most of the time. And many a mother has never been more glad for her child's continued nursing than when she had to help him through an illness or injury so severe that it required hospitalization.

Though little ones who are nursing do experience illness,

sometimes even severe illness, their time at the breast is an investment toward their good health. Your bloodstream and, to almost that same degree, your milk carry antibodies to the infectious diseases you have encountered. Researchers are discovering new immunological factors in the living fluid that is mother's milk at a breathtaking rate these days. One of the antibodies, IgG, is in a form that is destroyed by digestion. But others, such as IgA and certain human milk leukocytes, have been shown to be quite active in helping little ones fight off disease. IgA, by way of illustration, protects by serving as a potent barrier, preventing your nursing child from being infected by specific organisms through his intestinal tract.

At this time we do not know how much of your milk your child must be taking in order to receive an effective "dose" of immune globulins. Nor do we know exactly how long it is before the child's immune system is completely formed so that help from your milk is no longer needed. Still the advantage that nursing provides a child in warding off disease is apparent to those who watch children closely. The growth of the child's immune system, like all other growth, is probably ragged and unpredictable, and continued nursing seems to help by keeping the available immunities at a more even level during the period in which your child's own immune systems are developing.

No doubt as time goes on, more study of resistance to disease and the way your child utilizes the immune factors in your milk will give us a better understanding of the role of nursing in the reduction of incidence and severity of infection. Many mothers have commented on how much healthier their children were, referring not only to infections, but also to allergies, before weaning. In time the scientists will catch up with the "old wives," who have long warned against weaning in spring, knowing that nursing provided the child with protection against "summer complaint," diarrhea brought on by eating foods contaminated by bacteria in hot weather.

Allergy is a reason that some children nurse longer than a year, for some children are well past their first year before they are able to eat foods other than mother's milk without becoming ill. Children who cannot use cow's milk or other milk products especially benefit from extended nursing. Without their mother's milk they could be prone to nutritional deficiencies because of their inability to have access to the nutrients in other milks at such an early age. Interestingly enough we are also finding that children who are prone to allergy often refuse solids until later than other babies. To force foods other than mother's milk upon these children may subject them to allergic reactions which they seem to have been instinctively avoiding. For that rare child with severe allergies, the perfect food that mother can provide becomes his only food for as long as he needs it.

There is also a tendency for many children to take up thumb (or finger) sucking upon weaning—often as soon as weaning is initiated. Sucking thumbs or fingers can force the child's permanent teeth out of alignment if it persists into the school years, while nursing actually improves the dental arch. Many parents, therefore, are eager to minimize the child's need for such comfort by nursing as long as the child wants to nurse. I do say "minimize" and not "prevent" thumb or finger sucking, for some children who can nurse whenever they want still seem to need to have their hands in their mouths sometimes. Yet nursing will keep the need for extra sucking and mouthing as small as possible and thereby reduce or eliminate some of those expensive orthodontist bills later on.

HELP AGAINST SKIN DISORDERS

Your milk contains among other things fatty acids not available in other foods. These acids seem to be helpful to your child in forming the best possible tissues throughout his body. The one tissue in which the effect of these fatty acids is usually easy to observe is your child's smooth, silky skin.

As your nursling becomes a toddler it does not seem to take more than a very small quantity of your milk to maintain that marvelous, touchable skin that we so enjoy in nursing babies and children. Even those children who nurse only once a day usually keep their special skin softness.

Not only does your milk make your child feel good to you; it also helps your little one feel good to himself by avoiding or minimizing skin disorders to which he may be susceptible. It is not at all uncommon for children who are subject to some mild forms of eczema not to show any symptoms of the disorder until they are completely weaned. Whether prolonged nursing decreases the severity of eczema in these children we cannot say for certain. Many people believe it does. We can be sure, however, that nursing has postponed the problem until the child is more mature and can cope with it better.

WHEN A NURSING CHILD DOES BECOME ILL

Though your child's health is likely to be better than it would have been otherwise because she is nursing, there is still no way we know of to prevent illness completely. An additional advantage that the nursling has, besides the probable reduction in frequency and severity of illness, is her ability to nurse through what illness she does experience.

Very often children who are not feeling well cannot tolerate cow's milk and frequently will accept nothing except the breast. Many a mother of a non-nursing child, in order to keep him from becoming dehydrated with fever, has had to resort to feeding foods which she would, hopefully, rarely or never give to a healthy baby—sweet soft drinks or sugared gelatin. Recently pharmacy shelves have been filled with cases of electrolyte solutions to be fed to sick babies and children. These are no doubt an improvement over highly sugared fluids, but a baby cannot depend on them for more than a few days at the most.

The breastfed child who is too ill to take any other food will almost always nurse. Instead of running around fretting over what to give a feverish child to drink, the nursing mother can rock her child and nurse, knowing full well that no fluid on earth is more suitable for her child, and that nothing else will be more gently received by her child's struggling little body than her milk. One mother said, "When he was ill, nursing was his only comfort and his only nutrition. Nursing was my only comfort during his two bouts with pneumonia. It made me feel I was doing something during a time of waiting and feeling helpless."

Even following surgery or an intestinal upset so severe that the child cannot tolerate anything by mouth, the food he can handle first, well before any other food, is mother's milk. Mothers have often been surprised to find after a severe illness that their nursing children have lost very little weight.

Toddlers who do not feel well frequently refuse all nourishment besides nursing. Their return to nursing may be so complete for a few days that they even have the loose breast-milk stool of infancy. It is important whenever you think your nursing child has diarrhea to remember whether he has been eating the past few days and to remember the appearance and odor of the breast-milk stool. Many a child who has been well on the way to recovery from whatever made him return to normal nursing has been needlessly treated for diarrhea because his caretakers did not realize that loose stools are normal for any little person, of any age, who is taking only mother's milk.

Even when little ones have been cutting back considerably on their nursing, in times of illness mothers' bodies seem to respond astoundingly to their children's renewed need for milk. The ability to sustain her child completely when necessary is valuable in the early years of mothering. The ease of caring for a sick child through nursing and the rapidity with which these basically healthy little people usually bounce back on their mothers' milk seem like reason enough all by themselves not to abandon the nursing relationship before the child's maturation makes it necessary.

No doubt there are many still undiscovered chemical and biological properties of human milk which contribute to good health in our little ones. More beneficial factors in mother's milk are being found all the time. It is likely, however, that perhaps the most significant health benefit from mother's milk derives from how it is delivered. To the nursing child, milk is fed almost incidentally as part of a warm, loving embrace.

The child who is nursing has access to complete relief from the hurts, fears, and anxieties he encounters daily. The child who receives affection and a ready welcome into his mother's arms is likely to be a happy child, and it is becoming better known all the time that happiness, including good self-esteem and freedom from anxiety, is an irreplaceable ingredient for achieving and maintaining good health.

WHEN THERE ARE OLDER SIBLINGS

Mothers who have nursed one or more of their other children are almost always eager to repeat the experience with the next child. Most of us look forward to nursing again. Nursing requires us to take the time to build as special a relationship with the youngest as we did with the older one(s) when they were nursing.

Older siblings often seem to respect nursing time, especially if they have had the chance to outgrow their own need to nurse naturally. In fact they frequently insist that mother nurse a fussy or pesky little sister, usually out of concern for the needs she is expressing, though occasionally they just want her away from the block tower they are building. Mothers notice that older children often restrain themselves from interrupting their younger siblings' nursing times, while they will insist on being a part of almost anything else mother tries to undertake alone with the baby. So they especially appreciate nursing as a haven that is often, though not always, private, a haven in which they can give individual help to the newest person making his place in the family.

FUN AND GAMES

Nursing, happily, is not always a serious application of developmental psychology. It can be quite a fun time, full of play and humor. "I remember the little fun games of peek," one mother says, "and the adoring eyes looking back at me. I wouldn't trade those times for anything." There are memories of nursing a little cowboy with his hat and guns, a mechanic clutching hammer and screwdriver, or a little movie star in sunglasses. One tot parks her gum on mom's bra while she is nursing, but another forgot to take his gum out before nursing and got it stuck to mother.

Many toddlers learn to express mother's milk with little hands and react with surprise when they get a stream of milk in their faces—the same mix of surprise and pleasure that the farm cat shows when the farmer aims a stream of cow's milk her way. As comical as the games of squirting milk can be, however, mothers usually discourage them somewhat. We cannot always trust our children to be as selective as we would like them to be about whom to include as company for such games.

Nursing children are often quite aware of breasts and nipples. In many families little ones make a great joke of trying daddy's nipples. They may try to express milk from their own, and laugh and tease older siblings about their small nipples. One little guy pointed at the nipples of a large Buddha and gleefully squealed "nur-nur"! A small copy of "Venus de Milo" is very popular with the nurslings in my house. And more than one child has been seen trying to nurse from the *Playboy* centerfold. Parents get many laughs from their children's uninhibited and wholesome love of nursing and of breasts, even the parents of the nursing toddler who tried to help himself to what he thought was the main course in a topless restaurant!

OTHER ADVANTAGES

There are some lesser reasons which contribute to some mothers' decision to continue nursing past their child's first birthday. These include the use of breastfeeding as a tool in natural family planning, maintaining a milk supply for a baby expected through adoption, and keeping a nice bustline. One mother said she liked being able to take her little one with her everywhere using the excuse, "She won't take a bottle." Another said she found herself experiencing less anger toward her nursing child than toward her others.

Proceeding with last things first, many of us who spend most of our lives in padded bras thoroughly enjoy the larger breasts we have while nursing. Though desire for a better figure is a wish that is happily fulfilled through breastfeeding, it is hardly a sufficient motive to carry anyone over the inevitable rough spots. Larger breasts are just one nice fringe benefit. They do tend to last to some degree almost as long as nursing continues.

For a mother planning to nurse an adopted baby, having an established milk supply can be quite an advantage. It is usually somewhat easier to increase your milk when you are already lactating than to start from nothing. Still, you must be very thoughtful about your motivation in planning your care of one child to benefit the other. Nursing needs to be done primarily out of love and concern for the child who is nursing. Also you need to give careful consideration to the personality of your nursing child. Is yours a child who will be adaptable enough to allow you to care adequately for a new baby?

Do not read my words here as discouragement. I know

from my own family, which includes an adopted child, how satisfying and challenging it can be to mother one of these little people who need us so much. Every child and every situation is different, though, and the decision to adopt while your homemade child is still nursing is one that needs to be made thoughtfully, with a careful look at your own individual nursling.

There seems to be no need to worry, though, about forcing nursing to go on too long in your efforts to maintain a milk supply. Though it would not be advisable to press your child to nurse when he clearly does not want to, the supposed dangers of nursing too long just have not been documented. Besides, the experiences of so many mothers who did not want to wean when their children did lead me to wonder whether it is possible to coerce a child to nurse even if you should want to. Children who do not want to nurse will not do so. If your child still nurses willingly, there is no harm in continuing.

If you intend to use nursing as part of natural family planning, then you should assume that nursing will probably need to continue past your child's first birthday, and perhaps past her second. In order to be an effective means of contraception, breastfeeding needs to be part of an overall approach to child care which Sheila Kippley in her book *Breastfeeding and Natural Child Spacing* has named "natural mothering." For many mothers the infertility achieved through a thoroughly natural approach to breastfeeding lasts into the baby's second year or occasionally beyond. But even if for you fertility should return before your child's first birthday, you would hardly want to abandon suddenly the free and natural relationship you have developed with your child. Natural mothering, as Mrs. Kippley makes clear in her book, is a fine and rewarding objective in itself, and natural infertility is a bonus that many families enjoy. Prolonged nursing is usually part of that natural mothering.

Many mothers, even if they are not concerned with natural family planning, still enjoy the amenorrhea following childbirth that breastfeeding can produce. If you are interested in ways to maximize the time between childbirth and the resumption of menstruation, *Breastfeeding and Natural Child Spacing* provides the information you need. Mothers who are prone to anemia or troubled with hypoglycemia or premenstrual tension especially appreciate a long period of amenorrhea.

Like other simple reasons for nursing or for continuing to nurse past our society's norm, contraception or a time without menstrual cycles are not by themselves adequate motivations, but rather, like a nicer figure, fringe benefits. Nursing is a complex relationship, and our reasons for entering into such a relationship need to be an equally complex mixture of warmly irrational and coldly logical hopes and objectives. Such a mixture of heart and mind will enable us not only to overcome any obstacles we meet, but also to get maximum enjoyment out of an essentially pleasurable interaction.

WHEN EXPERIENCE SPEAKS

Most parents who have had the experience of caring for a nursing toddler cannot imagine rearing subsequent children any other way. Only four or five of the nearly one thousand mothers who wrote to me about nursing past one year said that they would not do so again. And the very few who did not want to repeat the experience were overwhelmed, not by nursing, but by the attitudes of other people who were against the nursing.

A few fortunate mothers have had even more than their own experience to help them enjoy a long nursing relationship. One mother says, "My mother nursed me until I was two, so I had a good backup source." Another wrote, "My grandmother and great-grandmother both nursed their children as long as the children wanted to nurse, and I received encouragement and support from both of them." People who have nursed well past infancy have learned in their own homes what a good thing extended nursing is and would rarely advocate any alternatives for themselves—or for their grandchildren. An increasing number of parents or grandparents will agree with the mother who wrote, "Of course I would nurse past infancy again—he turned out so cute and nice and smart," or the parents who said, "We found that the longer we nursed our kids, the better they turned out."

CHAPTER 3

Nursing
—Still the Best
for Your Child

EARLY WEANING—NOT RECOMMENDED FOR CHILDREN

The impression that most people unfamiliar with the concept of natural weaning have is that prolonged nursing will harm the child. Yet in truth we would have a hard time finding instances in which little ones are actually weaned for their own good. Only in the case of galactosemia in the infant, a condition so rare that I hesitate even to mention it, would nursing be harmful to the baby. The purposes for weaning at any specified age were thought up, not to help the child, but to relieve the mother of one of her jobs.

It is true that ever so many of us have weaned because we were convinced by someone that it was best for our babies. But if we had gone back to the origins of those reasons, we would find almost always that the real reason arose from an effort to make life easier for mom (or the pediatrician or grandmother or husband or whomever mom complained to when life with her toddler became wearing and difficult). There is just nothing in family experience to indicate that a child's life is improved in any way by premature weaning.

Making life easier for mom is a commendable goal, of course, and there is no need to make up all the reasons for weaning that we make up. When a mother gets tired of nursing and wants this part of her relationship with her toddler to be over, her feelings deserve respect, not judgment, from others. No mother should accept insult from anyone just because she wishes her child would wean. While it is constructive for us as mothers to help each other evaluate the nursing relationship from the child's viewpoint as well as the mother's, it is not ever constructive to label someone as a "good" or "bad" mother, even in our own minds, on the basis of nursing or weaning decisions.

If a mother can face weariness with the nursing relationship with a good store of self-respect, she will be in the best possible state of mind to evaluate the nursing relationship in which she is involved. Many mothers, seeing that the only real obstacle ahead in the course of nursing is the negative feelings they themselves may be experiencing, are able to relax and meet their little one's nursing needs in a casual way. They say to themselves, "Okay. After all, all people do wean eventually; I'll get my way in the end." As one mother who kept nursing freely said, "I would rather nursing had ended sooner by my child's choice, but it's no big trouble." Others seem to need to make an effort to change the nursing relationship in whatever ways are comfortable for their toddlers so that they can bring their own feelings to a manageable level.

What is not constructive is to hide or deny our feelings. To continue to nurse an older baby and hate it tends to become martyrdom—a poor basis for any family relationship.

Our society's approach has not been particularly honorable or constructive either. Trying to cover up our own feelings is damaging enough to ourselves, but the "for the child's own good" approach tends to spread beyond just this or that family. The directives to wean "for the sake of the child" are published by gossip and "experts" until mothers who are enjoying nursing begin to feel compelled to wean lest they harm their beloved children. How much better it would be if each of us who really wants to nurse or to wean would have the confidence to do what we and our toddlers want to do and not have to press others to follow the same course.

PROLONGED NURSING AND DEPENDENCY

Some published advice tells us that children who are not weaned (or left with baby sitters or taken to nursery school, or

. . .) will have difficulty becoming independent. Yet researchers experimenting with young animals have told us what
observant grandmothers have always known: The fearful,
clingy kids (by which I mean school-aged kids who should be
pretty sure of themselves most of the time) are usually the
ones who have been pushed into situations requiring too
much independence too soon.

John Bowlby in *Attachment* quotes research done by H. F.
Harlow that demonstrates dramatically the role that clinging,
dependent behavior plays in the ability of infant monkeys to
move away from mother, to explore, and to learn in new situations. Harlow's experiments also demonstrate clearly that
the reason clinging behavior occurs in these young animals is
not, as Freudian psychology suggests, that it is rewarded by
nursing. Clinging or "attachment" behavior is independent of
the source of food and grows from the essential need to cling
that the growing infant has.

> Two . . . experiments deal with a young monkey's behav-
> ior (i) when it is alarmed and (ii) when it is in a strange
> setting.
>   When an infant monkey brought up with a non-feeding
> cloth model [as surrogate mother] is alarmed, it at once
> seeks the model and clings to it (just as the wild monkey in
> similar circumstances at once seeks its mother and clings to
> her). Having done so the infant becomes less afraid and
> may even start to explore the hitherto alarming object.
> When a similar experiment is done with an infant brought
> up with a "lactating" wire model its behavior is quite dif-
> ferent: it does not seek the model, and instead remains
> scared and does not explore.
>   In the second experiment an infant monkey is placed in a
> strange test room . . . in which are a variety of "toys." So
> long as its cloth model is present the young monkey
> explores the toys, using the model as a base to which to
> return from time to time. In the absence of the model, how-
> ever, the infants would rush across the test room and throw
> themselves face downward, clutching their heads and bod-
> ies and screaming their distress. . . . The presence of the
> wire mother provided no more reassurance than no mother
> at all. Control tests on monkeys that from birth had known
> only a nursing wire mother revealed that even these infants
> showed no affection for her and obtained no comfort from
> her presence.

These experiments tend to support what many of us observe in the real laboratory—our own homes with our own children. When our children are able to cling or be close to us as they need (and for the preschool set this can include nursing), they usually behave better and pay more attention to growing and learning. They do not cling because their behavior may be reinforced by the good taste of mother's milk. They cling because that is a basic need in itself. When on the other hand we get preoccupied and are not as available to them as they need, they get cranky and waste much of their growing-up energy trying to get close to us and get our attention.

Experience as well as experiment points toward the conclusion that the best way to help our children grow toward emotional maturity—and emotional maturity includes a reasonable amount of independence—is to meet their needs to be dependent and clingy while the children are little. Unlike handing your child a bottle or a pacifier (which might be likened to feeding with a wire dummy), nursing goes a long way towards fulfilling your child's dependency needs. Just as experimenters report that monkeys that have something soft and comforting to cling to overcome fear more easily than monkeys that do not, so hundreds of mothers have reported to me their pleasure and pride in the independence and self-confidence of their nursing children.

The most common experience with nursing toddlers is the super-independent toddler—the one who tries everything, accepts more people without fear than might be usual in our culture for any particular age. Nursing mothers take credit for this fine emotional development, and most of this credit is deserved. The freely nursing toddler is getting the bulk of his dependency needs met and is going to show the independence his personality and development allow.

The last phrase above is something all of us parents need to recognize, so it might be good to re-read it. What you do with your child is very important in making independence possible. Your child, however, has a unique personality and timetable for development toward independence, and even in the best of emotional environments that timetable may be amazingly fast or painfully slow. One two-year-old is hysterical at the sight of a bug, but adores people—all people. Another plays with bugs, but is terrified of everyone, including grandma. Another is kind of in-between—bugs are okay; grandma and other "strangers" are okay at home, but not at grandma's house or the grocery store or anywhere else. I am very familiar with these particular variations, because these descriptions fit three of my own when they were nursing two- and three-year-olds.

Each child's special personality creates an individual pattern of fear and confidence at each age. We are learning the best ways to develop each child's confidence and overcome fear. We provide opportunities for children to enjoy their confidence. We make every effort to provide enough support (not excessive, of course, but generous—enough to make them feel protected) when they are afraid. A readily available source of comfort and support for a frightened little one is his mother's breast. For many children the more dangerous things (as they see danger, not necessarily as we see it) they may try to face, the more comforting and reassurance they will need, and this often includes more nursing.

As effective a source of comfort as nursing is for a frightened (or just tired and overextended) toddler, it is not really surprising that so many parents of nursing toddlers are really pleased with their children's independence. These children know that there is comfort for them if they meet fear or pain.

A significant minority of us have had the incredible experience of watching an extremely clingy little one at three, at four, and still at five (this kid is never going to grow up!) blossom into a little drill sergeant, a child who at seven dances before an audience which includes the governor, and more importantly, fellow second-graders, without a twinge of stage fright. Of course the possible need of the clingy toddler for several years of nursing is only a part of helping these little ones become self-sufficient. It is the experience of many families that these very, very disoriented little people are able to learn confidence, not by being forced into situations in which they are expected to function independently before they are ready, but by having their mothers close for as long as it takes for them to feel confident on their own. These children are clingy by nature—nursing does not make them this way. There is no doubt that nursing helps both mother and child grow through this time of life.

NURTURING INDEPENDENCE

The idea that children who are not weaned do not develop independence has grown from an observable fact. People must experience success at functioning independently in order to become independent. We need to make independence possible as soon as children can handle it. However, such experience is useful only when an individual is ready. Forcing independent behavior on a preschooler is just about as effective as forcing independent breathing on a premature baby. It can be done sometimes with lots of special know-how and equipment, but the risks are staggering.

One experimenter tried "teaching" independence to some puppies in a way that you have probably tried with your own child—not as harshly I assume, but in the same manner. The experimenter studied following behavior, which is one way the young, including our own children, show their dependency.*

> One group of puppies not only received no sort of reward but were punished each time they attempted to follow "so that their only experience with human contact was painful." After several weeks the experimenter stopped the punishment. The puppies soon ceased to run away from him and, furthermore, actually spent more time with him than did control puppies whose approaches had been rewarded with uniform petting and kindness (Bowlby).

The punishment did not serve to decrease dependency, but apparently actually increased it in the long run.

Similar experiments "punished" infant monkeys for clinging to their dummy "mothers" by blowing jets of air at them from inside the dummy. To escape the hated blasts of air the infants needed only to move away from the "mother." Yet the more they were discouraged from clinging by the annoying blasts, the more tightly they clung to the dummies.

These experiments have been repeated countless times with real youngsters by real mothers. Each of us has tried at some time or another to push away a child who wants to

*John Bowlby prefers the term "attachment" to "dependency" because of the value implications we give to the word "dependency," regarding it as less good than "independence."

nurse or cuddle just when we sit down in front of the TV with a bowl of soup in one hand and a cup of coffee in the other, or just when we have dumped those 500 buttons we ordered into our laps for sorting. Oh Mom, you should have known! The harder we push them away, the more persistently they struggle to get near. Our experience confirms what the experimenters observed in their laboratories. Pushing away does not teach independence; it teaches fear and desperate clinging. The independent child is the one who has been held close when that was what he needed.

Many, many mothers tell me how chaotic their lives have become when they were either ill or too busy with other things to nurse and/or cuddle freely. Others describe similar situations when they were encouraging weaning at a rate that must have been too fast for their little ones. Their children were fretful, clingy, mistrustful, and very demanding. When the mothers made themselves more readily available to their children, the children became happier and more independent again.

Abandonment (often suggested as a way of weaning— see Chapter 16) is not a good tool for teaching independence either. The child who needs mother very much, especially the child who is not wholly at ease with other caretakers, is likely to be devastated by her absence. René Spitz's classic film *Grief,* showing the shocking deterioration suffered by children left in hospitals without their mothers, should be required viewing for all who advise mothers to get their children independent all of a sudden by leaving them for a week.

A child is best equipped to develop the kind of independence that is based on faith that mother will always be there whenever he gets into a situation he cannot handle alone. The "escape clause" for the mother in this contract is the "situation he cannot handle" part. As each child grows older, there are fewer and fewer such situations. Provided your child is not prevented from exercising his developing capabilities, independence comes quite naturally with his increasing competence.

I have no doubt that youngsters need plenty of opportunity to succeed as capable and responsible persons. Still, it is clear that there is nothing to be gained by racing with your neighbors to have the most independent child who assumes the most responsibilities at the youngest possible age. There is much to be gained, on the other hand, by being available to meet your child's needs to be dependent for as long as he expresses such needs. There is much to be gained also by continuing to be available for nursing, since nursing allows you to meet his needs in so many ways. It helps you convince your child that the world is an okay place, that he has a home base as he begins to experience more and explore more. It helps him feel better when he faces disappointment, frustration, and pain while he is still growing his own mechanisms for dealing with these hard things.

If you put yourself in your child's place, you can see that it is very rough to grow toward independence if you have little relief from the bad feelings you face as a small person in a world built for big people. If you did not feel very much loved and protected, it would be ever so easy to lose that childish wonder and enthusiasm and just give in to fear and frustration. Things are so hard to do when you are little, and you get hurt so much. Nursing, rather than discouraging independence, can help it come more easily by providing the child a reliable way to soften her discouragement and fear in the difficult times.

DISCIPLINE WITHOUT WEANING

Many people regard the decision not to wean or not to toilet train or whatever as the beginning of a whole pattern of parenting that does not include discipline. Yet I do not understand how weaning (or toilet training) got to be a part of discipline. As I remember all that Latin I studied back in ancient times when people studied such things, discipline has to do with teaching, not with the arbitrary alteration of normal, natural behaviors. Discipline has to do with helping children develop into good, decent adults. To be well disciplined our children need to feel good about themselves and about their world. Then they need to be taught as much as we can teach them in the years they are under our influence about kind and courteous behavior. We must not try to force them to become socially acceptable too quickly, nor should we fail to challenge their growing consciences sufficiently. To go too far either way consistently (though we all stray one way or the other a bit almost daily) is to risk "spoiling" our children.

Closeness and loving, needed by all people, are critical to

little people. It is without closeness and loving, and without sufficient attention to the business of teaching good behavior, that children are spoiled. One mother tells me that things which are spoiled are things which have been left on the shelf to rot! Nursing does not contribute to such spoilage.

We do have to teach our children many things. At first, in our arms, we teach them that love is available from people—and we gently teach them whom to ask for love, and when, and how. Then as they move away from us we teach them how to behave so as not to hurt themselves or others. As time goes on we teach them not to annoy other people needlessly. Our efforts to teach care for themselves and courtesy towards others will not succeed right away, of course. As the well-known writer and educator Dr. James L. Hymes, Jr., describes discipline, we are beginning the years-long process of "doing a selling job on decency." Many actions that irritate other people may be unimportant, but we want our children in time to become conscious of people's feelings about their actions and how to evaluate behavior which may bother someone else.

Without attention to our children's need to learn how to receive love through an intimate relationship and to give love through slowly improving consideration for the feelings and property of other people—without such attention our children will be spoiled. You do not spoil a child by loving or by nursing—but by ignoring his needs for both love and guidance. Rather than setting the stage for undisciplined behavior, you can actually use continued nursing to help you create a more loving environment in which you can begin making your case for the decency which Dr. Hymes talks about.

NURSING AND SEXUAL DEVELOPMENT

A very common put-down handed parents of a nursing child, especially if that child is a boy, is that you are making your child homosexual. It is a very strange comment and hard to find a basis for. Weaning by or before one year is an unusual thing as far as human beings are concerned. We in Western society have had the longest and most widespread experience with early weaning (most of our babies were weaned at birth for quite a number of years). Yet it is our society which is so troubled over the question of homosexuality. Do we have more homosexuality in our early-weaning society? Or do we have factors unrelated to weaning patterns that contribute to homosexuality? Or is there merely something in the sexual mores we have developed that makes us worry about these things while other societies may take them as variations on the normal?

Dr. Niles Newton, a noted psychologist, reassured parents of sons who nurse longer than some people may think proper by pointing out that the valiant and virile Englishmen who defeated the Spanish Armada in 1588 were nursed for three years.

Dr. Newton went on to theorize that no one should worry about extended nursing making a boy homosexual. If anything, the nursing experience should encourage him toward heterosexuality by fixing him on the female.

She expressed surprise that our concern did not focus on the girl who nurses into childhood. Would her close physical relationship with her mother not predispose her to sexually intimate relationships with other women in the future? It seems logical that this might be true, but experience with now grown-up girls who nursed long and eagerly as little people has just not borne this out. Dr. Newton suggests the explanation that girls and women may not be sexually stimulated very much by what we see and therefore receive a different and entirely appropriate sexual imprinting at our mother's breast.

THE SENSUAL NATURE OF BREASTFEEDING

We have so sterilized and idealized nursing in our minds that many of us have lost sight of the fact that breastfeeding is a sensual behavior for both mother and baby—beautifully and wholesomely sensuous. Despite what our puritan background may shout at us from inside our heads, it is not bad for something to feel good. It is not bad for nursing to feel good to mother, nor is it bad for it to feel good to the child.

A child who is nursing without clothes on may sometimes explore with little hands any part of his or her body, including genitals. Now and then a mother is startled at seeing her son's little penis stiff and erect, or at seeing her daughter fingering her tiny nipples. These sensuous behaviors, however, do not portend any growing evil in our children. Rather they indicate that everything they will need for grown-up sexual behavior is there and in working order.

Sadly we cannot help sometimes regarding our children in adult terms. It is not always possible for us to see the sexual behavior of the very young as the childish activity that it is. There is no need to try to curb such activities in our children. But there is no need to watch it when it bothers us either. Any time you feel uneasy you should feel free to cover her with a blanket or to put his clothes on.

Mothers also sometimes become sexually excited while the baby is nursing, especially as their nurslings grow older and nurse less frequently. On rare occasion a mother has been said to experience orgasm while nursing. A mother should be reassured that such excitement is as normal as the reduced breast sensitivity some experience. It happens to almost all nursing mothers sometime or another—to some more than to others.

It can be rather upsetting to find yourself "turned on" if you are shy and do not expect to feel this way. There is nothing to be worried about, though, but rather much to be enjoyed. Because of your love and concern for your child you will be sure to make your outward reactions to your feelings of stimulation appropriate to your mother-child relationship—stroke his back, ruffle his hair, count her fingers and toes. But what goes on in your head when you feel this way cannot possibly hurt or confuse your child, and many mothers quickly learn just to sit back and enjoy the feelings.

Nor is it likely that you will experience feelings of sexual stimulation in embarrassing situations; most of us have to be in a very comfortable, intimate setting before we are able even to begin to feel aroused.

Some mothers have told me that sexual stimulation from nursing is one of its joys, not one of its problems. What a pleasant attitude! For the sensuous pleasure of nursing for mother and child is one way nature has insured that this vital activity will persist from generation to generation.

NIGHT NURSING—A FACTOR IN TOOTH DECAY?

Dentists have been troubled lately by what seems to be too many children developing cavities in their upper front teeth at an early age. There is reason to believe that there is a greater tendency for children to develop this particular pattern of tooth decay if they lie in bed at night with a bottle of milk or juice or (the dentist shudders) a sugary soft drink; for this reason such a pattern of decay has been named "bottle-mouth syndrome."

A few nursing children also have serious problems with tooth decay, and some of the first advice a mother gets is that she should stop all night nursings. There are a number of reasons to doubt, however, that night nursings contribute to tooth decay in these children. We do know that night nursings contribute to quiet in the household and that continued nursing contributes to the child's health in other ways. Besides, weaning from night nursings can be the most difficult weaning of all if the child is not ready.

It seems obvious that in this matter, as in others, we need to look at the whole child. The child is more than teeth. All too often dentists or pedodontists recommend weaning at night without any understanding of what such weaning will mean in the emotional development of the young child, especially in the child under two or so. If your child is attached to night feedings and threatens to destroy his sleep and yours if you try to change this important part of his life, then it is certainly time to weigh what you may hope to gain by night weaning against lost sleep and possible damage to good feelings between yourself and your child from trying to wean at night.

The first thing to remember when thinking about night nursing and tooth decay is that a huge majority of nursing babies and children do nurse at night, and few are troubled with much tooth decay. There is certainly no reason to worry about it at all unless your child is one of the few with the problem. Besides, it seems reasonable that nursing from the breast at night is less of a factor in tooth decay than would be nursing from a bottle. The child draws your nipple well into his mouth so that the milk is delivered far back in his mouth, against the soft palate. He gets much less of your milk on his teeth than does the baby sucking on a bottle. The bottle delivers milk much nearer the front of his mouth, thoroughly bathing his teeth in the sugared formula. Unlike the bottle, also, the breast does not drip into his mouth as the bottle does. He gets milk only when he is awake enough to suck and swallow, so that breast milk does not pool in his mouth as milk from a bottle would.

Many parents decide not to wean at night, even though advised to do so because of the child's severe tooth decay and have instead taken other less drastic measures to help protect their little one's teeth. First of all they realize how enormous a factor diet is in dental health. They do every sneaky thing they can to make whole, fresh, as-close-to-nature-as-possible foods become their children's favorites. Mothers who have always before been impatient with food fanatics find that this is the time to ban white flour and sugar from the family table, at least until the tooth problem is under control. They even say a sad farewell for now to nutritious but stick-to-the teeth favorites like dried fruit, raisins, and honey. They encourage instead frequent snacks of crunchy raw vegetables and whole fresh fruit like apples, knowing that these foods actually help clean the teeth.

Such changes in diet may be difficult, but at least they come in the daytime when everybody is awake. And, unlike weaning at night, this is a positive step which will not hurt anybody. Some of us parents may go into withdrawal symptoms for a while if there is no chocolate cake after supper, but we big guys can surely make a temporary sacrifice for a little guy. Besides, we too will be better off on this kind of diet.

Some people suggest following your child around with a toothbrush and brushing every time he eats anything (including after nursing). This has not been proved to be helpful though; after all, both severe tooth decay and tooth brushes are relatively modern phenomena. Some dentists say that if you do an expert job, one good brushing a day will do all that brushing can do. Your dentist can teach you how to do that expert brushing, so be sure to ask for instructions.

Above all, it seems hard to believe that something as time-tested and as linked with the survival of man as is breastfeeding could be harmful to any significant number of normal children. It would seem much more sensible to look at almost anything else in our children's lives for the explanation of tooth decay or any other problem before we would look at the age-old act of nursing, be it in the day or in the night.

NURSING AND WEIGHT GAIN

So often mothers have told me that they were advised to wean because their children were gaining too slowly. Every time I have been asked about this I have looked around for a thin, sickly child who obviously needed a change in diet. Every time instead I have seen a firm, nicely proportioned, healthy little child, usually, but not always, a two-year-old.

Children around the age of two are notorious for eating nothing, or so it seems to mother. (Actually they eat everything—you know, a dog biscuit, the last three drops out of your coffee cup, the little orange that was just beginning to ripen on your treasured miniature tree—everything except what is on their plates at mealtimes.) During this time in their lives, it should be more a comfort than a worry when a child has a regular source of nutritious food through nursing.

As if it were not enough that we parents may worry about the child who eats little at mealtime, we also may have to deal with relatives or friends who fret over their not eating. A mother who has faced the concern of others over her child's eating so little learned to tell people that he had just eaten a little while ago. "Most people accept that," she said. And in the case of a nursing toddler this statement is usually not a complete falsehood.

Many of us do worry about little children, though, especially little boys—the ones who do not weigh as much as the charts say they "should" or who are not "tall enough." Why do we think that smallness at two determines smallness at twenty? What is wrong with being small at twenty anyway? And, even if it is bad to grow up small, and being small at two means that is the way the child will grow up, what makes us think there is very much we can do about it? A healthy child who has access to food will take in all the calories he needs. If you make sure he can get a wide variety of foods, and this can include your milk, and do not let his taste get confused by sweets, you will not need to worry.

Look at your little child if you are worried about his weight and height. Think about the pictures of the starving children in . . . wherever. Do his bones stick out like that? How well can you see his ribs? If your child's outstretched hand has dimples at the knuckles, or if he has dimples at the back of his elbows or front of his knees, your child is officially cherubic and plump and may not be lined up with our skinny ones. Back to the really thin ones—and I am not expecting you to turn up a case of true starvation, nor will there even be a case of real undernourishment if you nurse without limit and make nutritious food available every few hours throughout the day—if we can learn to accept the fact that some children are short and some are thin and some are both, just as there are thin, short, and thin-short adults, we will be ever so much happier.

The nutritional problems that you read about which result in stunted growth or impaired brain development do not occur in babies or young children who are nursing, for children develop normally while they are receiving the superior protein in human milk. Problems develop, not from nursing, but upon weaning, if the foods available to the child, even though they may contain more than enough calories, do not contain adequate protein for continued growth and development. Poor sanitation in some countries also leads to more sickness in these children and compounds the ill effects of their inadequate diet (Robinson).

Fortunately, your child will not be at risk of stunted growth, physical or mental, no matter what anybody tells you, because you can easily manage to avoid such a deficient diet as nothing but millet or polished rice, the diet families must resort to in some places.

When you have a child who is smaller than "normal," however, you need as much support as possible to help you feel secure when someone, maybe even your doctor, gives you that psychologically devastating stab—"You are not giving your child enough to eat." You need to be reassured that a child must be rather severely deprived of nutritious foods over quite a period of time before any permanent harm is done. Since your child is receiving almost every one of the nutrients he needs from your milk alone, the odds are low indeed that he is malnourished. If you nurse freely and if food is where he can get it himself whenever he is hungry, it is quite unlikely that he is even undernourished. There are probably genetic reasons that have to do with growth patterns in your family and with how big your child will be as an adult which dictate that your child should be the size he is right now.

If your child is thin enough to worry you, you do need to make a thorough check of his health—is he anemic; has he picked up pinworms; is his thyroid normal, etc.? If all is well health-wise, then just enjoy how much easier it is to pick up your little lightweight, how much less damage he does when he jumps on your couch, etc. I'm sure you can think of many more advantages.

It does not make sense to wean a normal, healthy child merely in hopes of making him heavier or taller. Weaning probably will not affect his size—he is going to get heavier and taller anyway, but at his own pace, not yours. Besides, if you could make him get bigger faster, what would that accomplish?

You will notice that in speaking of older nurslings (older than nine to twelve months) I did not say that your milk contains all the nutrients your child needs. The one essential element not in your milk in large quantity is iron. The healthy, full-term baby has a store of iron in his liver that is sufficient for at least nine months, or even more. Recent studies also indicate that what little iron there is available in human milk seems to be absorbed more readily than iron from other sources, such as fruits, vegetables, or cereals (Finch).

A well-born baby has no need for sources of iron in his diet for nine months to a year provided he is breastfed. Some little people who were unusually sensitive to foods other than mother's milk have, without any sign of anemia, nursed exclusively even longer than a year without any other food.

Most babies, however, indicate a desire to taste other foods sometime in their second six months and are able to enjoy foods without problems. So most children are receiving adequate iron in their diet by the time their stored supply runs out.

If your child eats very little besides your milk, though, and is anywhere past his first birthday, you should be a bit thoughtful about iron. The little bit he eats should not be cheese or other dairy products which contribute nothing beyond what he is already getting from your milk. Foods available to him should be iron-rich and easy for people his age to eat. Foods that come to mind are tender meat, especially liver, eggs, raisins, dried apricots, and foods made with wheat germ including whole-grain breads. Some cereals are fortified with iron, too.

Except for making some iron-rich food attractive to your child in his second or third year, it is usually best to trust your child's preference for nursing or for eating other foods. Remember that some children who refuse foods other than mother's milk are allergy prone and seem to have food preferences that protect them from allergic symptoms.

The enormous concern lately about iron deficiency anemia in infants and young children results from problems which arise in formula-fed babies and toddlers who drink a large amount of cow's milk, not nursing babies and children. If you are selective about the foods that you offer to your nursing child, it is most unlikely that you will ever need to concern yourself about iron deficiency in his diet.

TOO FAT? TOO THIN?

It is hard to believe how often you will find in the same room people who feel pressured to wean a toddler who is "too small" and people who feel equally pressured to wean one who is "too fat." I do not know how nursing can be the cause of both problems—it seems that we would settle on one or the other. But either way, nursing—and nursing well into childhood—is the normal, natural thing to do. Any influence nursing has on your child's size is likely to be an influence toward being the size he is supposed to be.

Overweight in a toddler or older child can result from overzealous feeding—starting solids too early and the like. Either overweight or underweight are sometimes part of a child's natural growth pattern, but either one can also indicate a need to better the child's emotional environment through an improvement in the mother-child relationship.

If you are worried about whether you are creating an optimal situation for your child's rate of growth, think about some basic patterns. Are you nursing freely so that your thin child has access to plenty of milk or so that your chubby child does not insist on nursing extra frequently out of anxiety that you will say "No"? Are you over-using nursing many times each day to "plug up" your little one while you attend to your own thoughts and conversations? (We all do this some, and within reason it is fine; this is one of the happy conveniences of nursing past the first year, and especially during toddlerhood. Just don't overdo it.) Are foods readily available to your little child? Leaving food out the way you do for a cat is the only way to feed some active little people. Foods need to be easy to pick up with still awkward fingers. Many little ones hate being spoonfed and will begin to eat only when you put the food right on the clean table or high chair tray and let them do it themselves—almost always without the niceties of silverware.

You need to evaluate the kinds of foods that are left around or offered to your child. The sugar and white flour products should be under lock and key when you are worried about your child's being overweight. A heavy child also should definitely not be spoonfed; let her feed herself.

If baking makes you feel like a great wife and mother, perhaps it is time to forget cookies and desserts and concentrate on whole grain breads and main course soufflés. It is time to discover the joys of lean meats, raw vegetables, and grapefruit sections for snacks. A plump child has no need for whole cow's milk or for any milk but yours. (Skim milk is a poor food; better no milk at all than fat-free milk which is without the fat-soluble vitamins.) You should see that your child does not get an excess of sweet fruits, especially dried fruits, and balance these with a good mixture of less-sweet colorful treats like tomato wedges, carrot sticks, and strips of sweet red peppers.

If, once you have satisfied yourself that your child has a good nutritional environment—easy access to food, the right kinds of food, plenty of opportunity to nurse, and a reasonable level of "convenience nursing," your child is still "too small" or "too big," I would urge you to change only one more thing—that is how you describe your child's size. Say that he is "his size" or "her size" and enjoy the advantages the size gives you. Soak up the compliments that older people give you for your plump, healthy-looking child. In another time it was mostly the fat youngsters who survived, and you can enjoy the heritage of that time in the way so many people admire well-rounded preschoolers. Besides, a fat toddler who is well-mothered and offered proper nutrition will thin out in time. Or, parents of tiny people, think of the new clothes you can buy if your child can wear many of last winter's coats and overalls again with nothing more than a few altered hems and buttons. Relax and enjoy your child either way. Size is only one of the many things about him that are going to be decided by factors you do not control.

The one person, actually, who may get "too fat" with extended nursing is mother. It is such a pleasure when baby is little and nursing a lot to be able to eat heartily without gaining weight. If you are determined to stay slim, though, it will probably be necessary for you to reduce your food intake consciously and increase your exercise (not hard to do with an active toddler around) as your child nurses less and less frequently, especially after she becomes really interested in table foods.

CHAPTER 4

Nursing
—Still the Best
for Yourself

PHYSICAL EFFECTS OF NURSING

Most mothers at one time or another wonder whether continued nursing will drain their physical resources, weaken them, or make them prone to illness. Sometimes over-protective people, even medically trained people, suggest that this is so. But our bodies are designed for childbearing and nursing so that with reasonable care for ourselves neither pregnancy nor nursing need produce physical stress.

A few mothers, though this is quite uncommon, do tend to lose weight or have difficulty maintaining their weight toward the end of the first half year or year of nursing. But most mothers undergo no change in weight or gain just as they would if they were living and eating the same way without nursing. Only in a severely undernourished mother would there be need to worry about nursing's drain on her physical resources.

Even if you are one who experiences more weight loss than you like while nursing, there is no particular danger to you provided you are eating well and otherwise taking care of yourself. Fortunately you are not required as is a dairy cow to produce milk at maximum levels for as long as possible. You can safely devote your energies to the well-being of your baby or toddler. When in time your little one becomes more interested in other foods, she will need less of your milk, and your body will again be able to use the food you eat to rebuild whatever stores are natural for you.

Another concern a few people express has to do with mothers' low estrogen levels while nursing. One mother was even told by her physician that her uterus would atrophy if she kept nursing. Natural estrogen is actually at a lower level only during what is called the "lactation amenorrhea," the time from childbirth until menstruation resumes. This amenorrhea does not usually last until a child weans naturally (though in a few mothers it does).

Now and then a mother who does not menstruate for a year or more because of nursing may notice changes because of prolonged low estrogen levels such as vaginal dryness or itching. This condition can be relieved a bit with some of the vaginal creams available in pharmacies. A few physicians are prescribing estrogen ointments for mothers who complain of vaginal symptoms, and these products do eliminate the symptoms dramatically. But considering the possible long-term effects of the use of estrogens, more of which are being discovered daily, it seems to be quite risky to use such potent hormones.

The low levels of estrogen while nursing are natural. There is no reason to expect damage to the uterus or anything else from a normal, natural hormone state. Any possible discomfort disappears with the resumption of ovulation and menstruation.

Though there may be occasional discomfort, there is no significant direct physical drain from nursing as long as you have a reasonably good diet and enough rest most of the time. Mothering preschool children is quite a drain on mother, yet nursing is not an added drain, but one way to make that mothering job easier.

DEALING WITH YOUR OWN DOUBTS

Nursing past your child's first birthday, or second, or fourth—or whatever, depending on where you have put your own dividing line between confidence and doubt about your nursing relationship—is likely to be at least partly an intellectual decision. And like most things we decide in our heads to do as parents, it is hard for us to do it with complete confidence. Things we have seen done as we were growing up, especially patterns of parenting in our own childhood families, are the easiest for us to follow without doubt. Whenever we nurse longer than anyone we knew as we were growing up, we are going to feel unsure at times. Are we going to harm our precious children by making a bizarre, selfish, wrong choice about weaning?

When these doubts arise it is time to visit with mothers who are nursing or have nursed a child older than yours, and maybe even better, someone whose child nursed such a long time and is now growing up obviously okay. La Leche League is made up of mothers with many kinds and degrees of nursing experience and can be a good source of empathy and encouragement.

Another person to look to for feedback about continued nursing—the first person really—is your child. How does he feel about nursing? How would he react if you tried to stop nursing now? Your child's feelings about nursing were not learned out of a new book nor through conversations about nursing with the neighbors or La Leche League or anyone else. Your child's feelings about nursing are an expression of what is going on inside him. Though your decisions about life with your child will not be totally decided by his feelings, nonetheless his feelings do deserve a lot of consideration. If your child expresses a continuing need to nurse, you should weigh those expressions of need as a big part of your consideration of whether or not it is best for nursing to go on.

Doubts are greatest with the first child who nurses past our self-imposed limit. It is hard to believe, no matter how many people tell us, that little people do quit nursing, more or less on their own. Once we have experienced natural weaning, that doubt usually becomes much less urgent.

If you are nursing now and feeling uncertain whether it is best to continue, I really do not expect what I have to say to make you feel completely better. Almost all of us have to grow through the same sort of progress as did the mother who wrote: "Now that I'm older and more experienced . . . I am much more inclined to ignore remarks from friends, relatives, and doctors. But the first baby seemed such a terrible responsibility, and I wanted so much to do right by him." Some part of the equipment built into good parents keeps us questioning and evaluating what we are doing, especially during that first "experimental" time we try a new (to us anyway) approach in parenting. You will do best to realize that your doubts are completely normal. In fact they are solid evidence that you are a good parent on the way to becoming even better. You are watching and evaluating, striving to allow life for your child to be the best it can be. How fortunate your children are to have parents with doubts!

Do not let the doubts get bigger than you are, though. Talk with people who support your viewpoint—again let me recommend La Leche League. There you will probably find the people who can help you most—parents whose little ones have nursed longer than yours, no matter how long that may be. When you are feeling uncomfortable doubts about a parenting decision like continuing to nurse or not, expose yourself to people facing similar decisions. Bask in the warm support of those who are proceeding in a similar way. Give those who are making different choices a chance to "convert" you to what they are doing. You will feel better, enjoying closeness with those who agree with you, and a conviction that your decision is right for you since you have made it with full knowledge of differing viewpoints.

Most of all, though, you can overcome your doubts by looking at your child. Your happy, learning, growing child is evidence that you are doing fine. You are a good parent. Pat yourself on the back and feel proud.

COPING WITH FAMILY PRESSURE

You have the tools to deal with your own doubts when you have them—attacking doubt immediately by reaffirming your decision, or giving doubt a fair chance by re-thinking everything, or just deciding to live with doubt for a while to see what happens. You respond to your doubts differently at different times. Sometimes you use other people to help you feel better; sometimes you do it alone.

It is harder to handle our doubts if others around us express similar questions. Uneasy feelings we have been handling well break to the surface when someone dear to us, especially husband, talks about having the same uneasy feelings. The foundations of our decisions are suddenly undermined, and we tend to react with emotionally charged defenses. We often interpret our mates' doubts as an attack on our ability to make decisions.

It can help so much to keep in mind that the people we love usually have the same kinds of concerns for our children that we do. They go through the same kinds of worrying and questioning that we do—maybe not as much or as soon in some instances, but the same kind. Keep in mind when your husband says, "If he's two (or "three" or "five") and still nursing, he probably won't ever quit if you don't make him quit," that not too long ago that is probably where you were in your own thinking.

If someone very close to you, husband being the most common example, seems to feel that you should discontinue nursing, be sure to acknowledge that he is concerned, as you are, about what is best for your child. Know in your own mind, and let him know you know, that his suggestions are made out of love for your child, not as an attack on you. Talk about your own doubts—ones you had in the past, and ones you still have. Do this slowly; let him see how much you have thought about it. Listen to what he has to say carefully and thoughtfully.

Talk about how you arrived at the decisions you have made. Take your time, and give him time. Try to explain your reasons step by step. Give him a chance to think without threat, listening to what he says. He does not have a chance to come around to your way of thinking if you consistently do what I all too often tend to do—get mad and shriek out the whole thing in under two minutes. I hope you will behave better than I do.

Dr. Gregory White suggests, though, that it is not always bad to react emotionally. "There are times when one good 'explosion' goes further than hours of reasoning," he says.

It can also be helpful when you are around members of the family who might not be at ease in the presence of a nursing couple not to nurse too openly right at first, especially with the amount of breast exposure we are comfortable with at home. We need to nurse quite inconspicuously in the beginning around certain people, sometimes even with our husbands or parents. Too much nudity too soon may be part of what causes some new grandfathers to find their daughters' nursing so distasteful. Of course we want to be able to relax and nurse in any way that is comfortable at home, but it is a good investment in the future of your nursing and family relationships to exercise discretion while the people who love you are coming to terms in their own minds with the way you have chosen to mother your baby.

Few of our family members have the kind of understanding of and encouragement for extended nursing that we have. We are fortunate to be, most of us at any rate, in contact with other mothers nursing into and past toddlerhood.

People near us, therefore, need to have us understand their feelings, too—sometimes before we can ask them to understand ours. In some instances it may be possible to improve the situation through the kind of empathy shown by the woman who wrote: "I helped my mother-in-law overcome her feelings of failure about not being able to nurse my husband as a baby. We talked about how few could succeed at nursing with the conditions she had in the hospital (ten days there, no nursing for the first two, rigid schedule, no night feedings). When she realized that she had tried and had not been at fault she could more easily accept my success at nursing." This grandmother had probably never before had her mothering efforts so accepted and affirmed by another mother, and it is no wonder that afterwards she had much greater faith in her daughter-in-law's ability to make mature and loving mothering choices of her own.

In general, though, we should not expect people whose peer groups are oriented toward eliminating baby "habits" as soon as possible to feel good about extended nursing right away. How did you feel the first time you saw a nursing toddler? How long was it before you could think of nursing so long yourself? Do not be surprised that, like you, the other people who love your child need a while to ask questions and to satisfy themselves that you have made the best possible plans in your child's best interests. Husbands deserve special patience and attention, because without their support, enjoying the nursing relationship is almost impossible. Besides, fathers are parents, too! They have parent's rights to help determine how their children are reared.

COPING WITH PRESSURE FROM OUTSIDERS

It is obvious that we can use patient discussion only with people with whom we can spend a great deal of time. The time we have with many of the people whose opinions are important to us is just too limited. Sadly, all too often we find ourselves blurting out a condensed version of our reasoning with these people and come out sounding like zealots on soapboxes. Or the end of a visit will come and close our discussion at an uneasy point, before we can even understand each other, much less come to some kind of consensus.

There is no greater cause of weaning than the effect upon us of other people's opinions. Parents have forced weaning upon toddlers so often because of an embarrassing incident that involved other people—a three-year-old insisting upon his bedtime nursing when there was company, or a two-year-old demanding to nurse at church, and the like. What a shame it is that so many young parents say they are glad to have moved across country or spent time overseas just because it enables them to live better, away from critical relatives.

Almost the only reason given by those few mothers who would not plan to nurse future children past infancy is along this line: "What other people think bothers me too much." Nursing is not the problem, but what other people think of it. "If we lived on an island," one perplexed mother said, "where nobody else cared what we did, I would let her nurse as long as she wanted. . . . I know one thing for sure: My baby is a lot more independent than I am." Though it surely can be difficult, we need to trust our own natural instincts as fully as our children do.

Many mothers have indeed learned to tune out criticism of their continued nursing, change the subject, and enjoy the company of dear people in other ways. As one perceptive father pointed out, what most people express is not disapproval of extended nursing anyway; it is just surprise.

Facetious answers are sometimes enough too, when they are offered in good humor and love, as with the mother with the toddler at her breast who was asked, "How long do you expect him to keep that up?" "Oh, another five minutes or so," she replied. A few people are satisfied once you remind them how long many children use bottles, pacifiers, or thumbs. Another way to circumvent critical or surprised comments is to say, "Yes, we're getting more and more involved with weaning these days," and then talk about something else.

Ducking the issue is not always the best approach, though, and you can tell right away when it's wrong. Some people really want to talk about weaning and will not let you change the subject. Other times you feel in yourself a strong need for that person's approval, so you really want to talk about it.

When discussion time is limited—when, unlike time with your mate, you do not have the evenings after supper, long chats over coffee, or the 2 A.M. "redeye specials"—there is probably no reason for getting into a debate. There is no chance for both of you to present all the facts and feelings each of you have so that you can examine them all and approach some kind of understanding. Besides, you have no need to "convert" everyone to your viewpoint. Instead you need to solicit their support and love for you as a person and their patience with the decisions you make as a parent.

Tell your mother-in-law or your sister who lives so far away—or whomever—how much you rely on her support for you as a parent. Tell her you know how much she cares for you and your child and wants things to be the best they can be for both of you. (Do not omit talking about either of the above two things: They are necessary proof that you are listening and that you care about her, too.) Remind her that you are also acting on your enormous concern for your child's well-being. You have learned from the experiences of other mothers you know and from reading, and what you have learned makes you sure than no harm comes from continuing to nurse.

Without going into endless detail, point out that you know some good comes from extended nursing. Emphasize the enjoyable parts of your continuing nursing relationship. Save your complaints for someone who can support you. Most people will respect your informed decision; they want to be helpful and feel a need to be sure this is not just a "bad habit" you have slipped into without thinking.

THE PERSISTENT CRITIC

Some few people it is sad to say, even with such a kindly worded, direct plea for love and support, or at least to tolerance, feel an urgent need to talk you into weaning and continue to do so at every opportunity. These people are often genuinely alarmed at what you are doing, though some older people are not so much alarmed by what you are doing per se as they are by the very fact that you, still a baby in their eyes, are a parent at all. Other people nearer your own age may need to put down your decisions as defense for their own parenting choices on the assumption that one of you has to be wrong. (How much better it would be if we could, every one of us, think through what seems right and feels right for our own families and then be neither threatened nor threatening when the neighbors do not make the identical decisions!)

Sometimes, if a person keeps offering unsolicited advice to the point that it is annoying you or your family, it becomes necessary to be very firm. One mother dealt with such a situation within her family by leaving the room for ten minutes when the subject came up. If it came up again, she left for twenty minutes, and so on until the criticism stopped altogether. Usually it is best, though, to talk about the problem. "I know many people who feel as you do about weaning. I've thought about it a lot, though, and decided to wean my own way. I really don't want to talk about it any more, please." By all means, stop the conversation about weaning there and go on to something else.

Now and then a friendship will seem to flounder because of how the friends feel about your nursing your toddler. If you are able to be easygoing about nursing, not defensive, then it is unlikely that a friendship would wane just because of your nursing. There may be other wedges between you, and your decision not to wean your child may be the final excuse for drifting apart. When you have a stable friendship you will be able to help your friends understand, or at least to accept your decision. It is usually possible to say, as one mother does, "Friends accept his nursing. Some are a little amazed that I am such a good 'cow,' but my friends, my son, and I have grown together." True friends are like that; less flexible friendships are usually no great loss.

There is one circumstance in which people criticize mothers for nursing, no matter what the age of the baby or child, and correctly so. Your neighbor or pediatrician or husband's secretary are absolutely right when they say that you should never nurse while driving. There is some, probably acceptable, risk in nursing when you and your child are passengers in a car, for he may bite you hard in the event of a sudden stop. But as a passenger you can minimize other, greater risks by making sure both you and your child are using adequate safety restraints while nursing. And, provided we make good use of safety equipment for ourselves and our children, it seems worth what small danger remains to be able to keep our nurslings calm and happy while we are on the road.

To nurse while driving, however, is to take too great a risk with your child's life. Besides your decreased ability to concentrate on your driving while your child is nursing, there is the very real possibility that he'll grab the steering wheel or lean against it with his body, throwing your car out of control. Moreover, in case of a collision, your child is in an incredibly dangerous place, likely to be crushed between your chest and the steering wheel. At highway speeds even a shoulder belt cannot protect your child from the force of your body hurled forward in a crash. For this reason if you are driving and need to nurse, you should always stop the car and change drivers or finish nursing before you go on. Though this may mean a loss of time, it is time you owe to your child, to yourself, and to the other people on the road that day.

WHEN YOUR CHILD RECEIVES CRITICISM OR TEASING

Now and then a person will criticize your continued nursing by teasing your child. In the situation in which people criticize you directly, you have the option of just ignoring what they say if it is not making you uncomfortable, or you can choose to respond. If your child is being used as a middleman, however, you must intervene for your child's sake.

Even questions in your child's presence may be best met with, "That's private, and I'd rather not discuss it now." Help the critical person see how unsettling it can be for a little person to face teasing for something that just comes naturally to him. It could also be enlightening to the critic if you point out to him or her that such comments are likely to put up barriers between the person and the child that could interfere with their future relationship. You can be kind and warm with your "critic," but you must also be as firm as you have to be. Do not allow the teasing to happen again.

Children still will be aware of some of the negative opinions others have about their continued nursing. "You know, Mommy," one four-year-old observed, "I think Daddy's afraid I won't grow up." But as long as your child does not have to face a direct attack from those who disapprove, you can reassure him that he is fine and that not everyone has to agree on everything. With your help the opinions of others will not trouble him much.

KEEPING NURSING PRIVATE

I have left until last the most satisfactory tool for dealing with people who might pressure you toward weaning before you want to—a closed mouth (and blouse). The older your child gets, the fewer the people who need to know you are still nursing. How often we suffer after volunteering personal, private information to people who had no need to know it! Sometimes you can even avoid answering a direct question from somebody you would prefer not to know that your child still nurses by giving a silly or ambiguous response. For the most part, though, people who think your child should be weaned will assume he is weaned unless you tell them otherwise. It is not even necessary to tell medical advisors that your child nurses if they would be inclined to criticize you, that is provided the nursing is not significant in evaluating a health problem. Otherwise, there is no need to set yourself up for comment when you want none. (On the other hand, when you do feel very self-assured, it is a good thing for you to let these people know that your child is not yet weaned. In this way doctors and nurses will in time come to realize what fine healthy children our little nurslings are!)

SEEKING SUPPORT AND APPROVAL

We all need support and approval from other people in our parenting roles. After all, we are novices at the job, especially those of us with small families. When we need encouragement and a pat on the back for nursing, as we all do from time to time, we should seek these goodies from people who are enthusiastic about nursing. We make trouble for ourselves by seeking approval from people for things they are not likely to understand or are not likely to applaud. When we need approval and encouragement from a beloved friend or relative, it is far wiser to seek their praise for things they are enthusiastic about, even if it is only our choice of laundry detergent or our little one's new haircut. We are foolish when we ask them to support us or praise us for decisions they are ill-prepared to understand.

We especially tend to misuse and misinterpret the help and advice we get from doctors and nurses. So often we expect our children's checkups to provide us not only with assurance that our children are healthy, but also with an "official" certificate of our good performance as parents. Our expectations put additional pressures on our medical helpers. Doctors and nurses are trained in identifying and treating illness. It is not fair to them to expect them also to be expert in all aspects of child care and family living. Besides putting pressure on doctors and nurses to be everything and know everything, asking them for advice on matters beyond their training can lead us to dissappointment. We find that their advice on child care tends to be no better and no worse than that of other reasonably well-informed adults. This is as it should be, but we set ourselves up for a letdown by expecting more.

I must add that, being just as human as the rest of us, doctors and nurses are also just as likely as anyone else to offer unsolicited advice on child care. Nor do years of studying pathology give them any better basis for counseling in child care than do years of studying computer science. What will qualify medical people to give good advice about child care is good family experience of their own. Because of such good experience at home, many medical people give excellent advice on life with little ones. So do many computer scientists. It is up to you to evaluate the advice you get very carefully according to what makes sense to you. As much as we might wish it to be otherwise, the world is provided with few, if any, physicians of the Marcus Welby type—that fictitious character who seems to be able to know everything about every patient and to be totally helpful and right all the time.

NURSING WHEN OTHER PEOPLE ARE AROUND

Maintaining that "closed blouse" I mentioned is not always possible around people, especially with the younger toddler. They can choose some of the most awkward company in

Gee, Lady, you must have hit him over the
head to make him stop crying so fast!

which to be overcome with the need to nurse. Many of these little people are so active, picking up your blouse to see if the other breast is still there, running their hands down the front of your shirt, etc., that nursing inconspicuously is much more difficult than when they were tiny. A vivid memory I have is of being in the back of a small Jeep on one of those Rocky Mountain tours. I was sitting knee to knee with some true-to-the-stereotype (you've got to believe me) Texas oil people and their teenagers. Throughout the tour I coped well with nursing our tiny new baby off and on. Before it was over, though, our toddler decided she needed to nurse, too. Now, that scene fits my personal definition of an awkward place and company for nursing a toddler! We did survive, and without red faces, because of following several guidelines in living with a nursing toddler.

First of all it is essential to plan ahead. As your child grows older you need to pay attention to your clothing with regard to what kind of closure your bright little tot is learning to operate. Many a mother has not thought of this until after the first time she has looked down to discover her zip-front being unzipped by the innocent angel in her arms. This is a

situation that calls for the temporary retirement of such clothing in the weeks ahead, and some immediate tickling and
other distraction at the moment until you can get away and
nurse.

For the first two or three years little people can be expected to ask to nurse anywhere the spirit moves them, and
often their articulation far exceeds their sense of what is and is
not socially acceptable. It is very difficult to keep nursing a
private matter when your child announces "I want to nurse."
"How cute!" remarked an aunt when a child made such a
request, "He still remembers." "How could he forget—it's
only been four hours," his mother thought to herself.

It can be really cute when little Lucy asks for "titty" or
"boobie juice" at home. Think, however, whether you are
comfortable having her make the same request in perfect
English at the supermarket. What word will be best for you if
your child should do what one New Zealand youngster did,
patting his mother's jersey and announcing to all around,
"Mummy has drinkies"? Will it be comfortable for you if your
three-year-old says "Mamma, get those nursers out"? How
will your word sound to you shrilled above the strains of
Lohengrin at a cousin's wedding?

This is not to say that your nursing relationship must be
secret or that there is anything wrong with any term whatso-
ever that you may want to use for nursing. I just want to alert
you to the fact that the word you use in the first or second year
will usually be the word your child continues to use, and the
pronunciation will become increasingly distinct. Though it is
possible to re-teach your child a new word later, it can be
quite difficult. So plan now, based on what will be comfortable to you.

Many families prefer to choose a "code word" for nursing. Since the "n" sounds come very early for many babies,
the "n" words are very common code words ("Ninny,"
"Nanny," "Num-Num," etc.). When the child starts saying
something repeatedly in babbling, you can pick up the
"word" and begin to use it to mean nursing. Some are real
words connected with breasts and nursing, words like "Snug-
gle," "All-Gone," "Jug," "Side." Others are baby sounds
turned into a code word like "Dee-Dee," "Yum-Yum," "Ne-
wee," "Mim," "Nummies," "Nur-Nur," "Nurney," "Brr-
Brr." Nursing in one Kansas household became "Oh," a
baby-shortened form of "Some Mo'." In another family nurs-

ing became "Mona" (Spanish for monkey) after the toddler saw a monkey nursing on television. Yet another family called nursing "Night-Night" and enjoyed the reaction of people when their "good" little child asked for "Night-Night" all by herself.

The advantage of the code word is that it is not a word in anyone else's language—just yours. In a crowded Jeep, or during a wedding processional it becomes just child noise to the uninitiated and gives you a chance to handle the situation in the way that is most comfortable for you. In our case in the Jeep, the driver asked whether "Nanny" was her doll, to which I replied, "No." Though she said frequently, "I want my nanny," she did not become frantic, and we made it through the remainder of the tour and into the privacy of our own car.

Often as your child gets older your wonderful private word for nursing will make it possible to use the next tool you can try—a tool I used in the Jeep—for avoiding embarrassment: Try side-stepping nursing in situations that make you uncomfortable. Distraction often helps a toddler wait—walking around jiggling, tickling, looking at new objects or toys. A verbal toddler can learn to go along with "Wait until we get home," or "After I'm through eating," or some such. A young child can learn where nursing is or is not appropriate and sometimes will accept a signal—such as your wearing a dress that fastens up the back on occasions when you don't want to nurse.

Do keep in mind, though, that avoidance, used very often, will add up to an initiation of weaning by you. You need to realize that if you find yourself delaying nursing, say for an hour or more, once a day, you are in the exact pattern so often recommended for weaning. If your child is not ready for weaning, the whole procedure could give you a result just the opposite of what you want—an increase in your child's request for nursing at times you find embarrassing.

Avoidance of nursing in certain situations is fine, of course. To keep from setting up a weaning atmosphere, though, it is helpful to remember when we have distracted a little one from nursing and try to be quick to respond to the next request. If you've promised to nurse when you get home or after supper, by all means do so. Your credibility is at stake. So offer to nurse at the agreed-upon time, even if he has forgotten about it.

Times arise, of course, especially with young toddlers, when their need to nurse is urgent, no matter how embarrassing you may find it to nurse right then. Many a mother in this type of situation has excused herself to "change a diaper" or "read a bedtime story" or "just to calm her down a little bit." There is no need to explain what you really do once the door is closed behind you.

You can occasionally avoid the need to nurse over a relatively short period of time, such as a trip to the grocery store or a brief visit at a neighbor's by planning ahead a bit. Your child may find it easier to go without nursing on these occasions if he is able to nurse just before you go.

If you cannot head off this request to nurse or excuse yourself and your child for a few minutes, or if you would prefer not to, then use all the sneaky, unobtrusive nursing techniques you have been using all along—pull-up tops, or dresses with secret openings, your hair (if it is very long) helping to cover up. A dress with hidden zippers is especially helpful with a child who likes to pull your shirt up high while nursing; with the small zipper openings, he cannot "overexpose" you. A poncho serves as a good cover-up at outdoor events. If you can lift your bra rather than having to unfasten the cup, it is easier to hide what you are doing. (Whether you can do this depends of course on how your bra is made and also on the size of your breasts.) If you do open the cup of your bra, you can usually put off fumbling with the closure— the hard part with most bras—until you are in private.

You may be able to persuade your toddler to be satisfied with one breast at times like these. Switching sides is just one more bit of commotion to call attention to what you are doing.

There will still be times when you have to cope with questions or stares you would rather not have come your way. But you can keep these uncomfortable times to a minimum while doing your best to meet the needs that your growing child has. Besides, it is fortifying to think that every time you answer a question or comment about nursing with warmth unsullied by evangelistic zeal, you bring just a little bit closer the day when what you are doing will no longer attract stares or comments.

CHAPTER 5

A Glimpse of Other Times and Cultures

Nursing a walking child has become so uncommon in the Western world that we do tend to regard it as a novel innovation. Yet according to Alan Berg, author of *The Nutrition Factor*, among the roots of our culture is a tradition of several years at the breast. The prophets of ancient Israel, as well as the merchants and the shepherds, were not weaned *before* two years. (Emphasis mine.) If Moses' mother was bound by ancient Egyptian customs as she reared her son to be part of the Egyptian royal family, she nursed him for three years. In ancient India, influenced by the belief that the longer a child nursed the longer he would live, mothers usually nursed their children as long as possible, often seven, or even nine years sometimes.

Nor have English-speaking mothers always weaned as early as we do in the twentieth century. According to Alice Judson Ryerson, who studied the kind of advice doctors were giving mothers about child care from 1550 to 1900, it was not until 1800 that most of the popular English writings on child care recommended weaning as young as twelve months. Even in 1725 writers commented on nursing four-year-olds with disapproval, an indication that a significant number of eighteenth century four-year-olds were still receiving love and comfort at their mother's breast. By 1850 most "experts" were recommending weaning by eleven months. At this time it was the nursing two-year-olds seen by child care advisors who drew official frowns. It is enlightening how closely these changes in recommended patterns of child care parallel other changes in family life that accompanied the Industrial Revolution in England and the United States.

Western culture did not overspread the whole world in one flash, fortunately. It took time for mothers' instincts to fall under the blade of progress. Early in this century Berg says that mothers in China and Japan still nursed their little ones for four or five years. During World War II Burmese children were happily at their mother's breast for three or four years. As Americans began the supposedly Fabulous Fifties, little people in Kenya could soothe their hurts and frustrations by nursing as long as five years.

In 1935 Margaret Mead says of the Arapesh, whose lifestyle she studied and described in detail, that the children nursed until the mother became pregnant again, not uncommonly until three or four. Other studies in the 1950s describe cultures not yet influenced by Western ideas. The primitive Siriono in Bolivia seldom if ever wean before three, and sometimes continue nursing for four or five years. In Tsinghai, China, mothers observed in 1956 were still nursing for several years, five years not being unusual, or until another child was born. In Inner Mongolia in 1951 children nursed two or three years, nor was it rare that a six- or seven-year-old would want to nurse a bit for reassurance. A study done in 1945 of sixty-four primitive cultures found only one in which it was clear that a child was ever weaned as young as six months.

In the 1960s extended nursing was still common enough among the Enga people in the Highlands of New Guinea that Thelma Becroft was able to conduct a most informative study of the quantity of milk mothers produce at different times during an extended nursing career. Children in the study were nursing freely and naturally at mostly two and three, but some at four years old.

Today, fortunately, Western weaning patterns are still not accepted worldwide. Dr. T. Berry Brazelton says of the isolated Zinacanteco Indians, descendents of the Mayas in the state of Chiapas, Mexico: When a new baby is born, if the mother "has older children, she continues to nurse them with the right breast, saving the left one for the new baby. Often a two-year-old and the infant will nurse simultaneously. By the age of four or five, children will no longer come to breastfeed at the mother's command, but before that they are expected to respond three or four times a day."

Nursing a toddler may seem unheard of these days in the U.S.A. or England or Rhodesia as mothers have written to me, and also in Germany or even in Sweden. Still, mothers who have lived recently in East Africa have been gratified to find that nursing for several years is still not rare there. Two North American women, one who had lived in New Guinea, the other in the Philippines, were pleased to see nursing extend naturally and lovingly past babyhood. A mother in Sweden writes of being blessed with support for her own extended nursing from an experienced mother of her husband's home country, India. "She said that in her country it is minimum with two years if mother and child both want it, and usually for another couple of years. Her husband, she told me, had been nursed for seven years."

This is not intended to be anything like a complete account of nursing and weaning patterns around the world past and present, though such an account would indeed be interesting. Rather I have given a few examples from published articles and from my correspondence to let you know that when it comes to extended nursing you are not alone.

Knowing that people in ancient or primitive cultures do something is not, of course, reason in itself to adopt that part of the lifestyle for ourselves. Ancient customs are sometimes abandoned for better ones, and some customs of primitive peoples serve to keep them primitive. The experience of other cultures does give us helpful information, but we must evaluate any practice we are considering on its own merits.

Yet knowing that in the not too distant past nursing almost always continued well past infancy is proof that extended nursing is not debilitating in any significant way. Any serious harmful effects of long-term nursing would have crippled the entire ancient world. Knowing that children no longer babies still nurse in primitive communities around the world today gives us a feeling of sisterhood and continuity in our mothering style. For, though we have broken away from the childbearing patterns of the immediate past, we join with the mothers of those cultures who can carry the tradition of tender nurturing for the young from antiquity on through the twentieth century.

PART II

Nursing
Your
Toddler
—How?

CHAPTER 6

Marriage and Life
With a
Nursing Toddler

CHANGES IN SEXUAL INTEREST

It worries me a bit to think of everybody who turns to this chapter looking for some definitive statements about how the relationships within marriage, especially sexual relationships, are affected by nursing and how to deal with these effects. There are many people now actively researching marriage and how it works, especially concentrating on human sexuality. (I am not one of them.) These people have no definitive statements about nursing in this context, or perhaps I should say that the definitive statements that they make seem to contradict each other. So common sense will have to tide us over until someone comes up with satisfactory answers to all our questions.

There is little need to discuss relationships other than those in which people have lowered sexual interest, for in our society these days it is when we are less interested in sex that we begin to have that "What's wrong with me?" feeling. A generation or two ago people worried when they thought they had too much interest in sex, but all this is part of our cultural pendulum ride. I do want to be sure to say to those couples whose sexual feelings are unchanged or enhanced when there is a nursling in the family that you are not at all unusual. You are among the fortunate many. The way you feel is great—enjoy this time in your life. Skip this chapter (and what a lot of other writers have to say, too). Like the old poem's centipede who was able to walk happily only until the time she was asked "which leg comes after which," it is possible to think so much about something which is normal and natural that you lose it.

On sex and nursing, there is no clear evidence that nursing itself affects sexuality. There are families in which at night the husband "takes up where the baby leaves off," and that is that. Some people say that the low levels of estrogen we have following childbirth up until the time we resume menstruation may decrease interest in sexual play, but research with sexually active post-menopausal women (who also have low estrogen levels) seems to rule out this assumption.

It may seem logical that one way nature might help protect the new baby from being followed too closely by another baby could be to reduce the new mother's interest in sexual intercourse. But total nursing itself provides a lot of protection against closely spaced pregnancies, and there is no evidence that lowered sexual interest in new mothers is part of nature's family planning. In fact, the truth is that there are women— and no small number either—who have an increased sexual desire immediately following childbirth.

Our attitudes toward nursing—and here I am talking about both husbands and wives—probably exert a much greater influence on our sexual feelings than do any other factors such as hormone changes. Do we see ourselves and each other differently because of nursing?

I found it unsettling once in a group of couples to hear the men describe their wives' nursing. Husband after husband described his wife as a madonna. The Madonna and Child do make a beautiful tableau, and we women put ourselves into that picture, too, though few of us would confess to our vanity. I wondered at that time, though, how many couples in that group were inhibited by the fact that in our culture the Madonna is the Virgin. The Virgin represents many wonderful things; but sexually she is strictly off limits, and that is significant. There is nothing wrong in seeing ourselves or being seen by our mates as a madonna. The problem is in our ability to switch from the virgin and her consort to Caesar and Cleopatra when we want to. Either parent, or both, may find it hard to switch images or may not even be aware of the need to try.

If we experience sexual effects from some of our images of the nursing mother, overcoming these effects will take patience and time and conversation. It may help a father or mother to read accounts of lusty ladies who nurse their little ones. The nursing mothers in Pearl S. Buck's *The Good Earth* and *Sons* come to mind. Some of the old Dutch painters like Jan Steen portray beautiful, robust mothers who clearly do not fit the madonna image. There are also quite a number of sexy screen stars who nurse their babies. All this, of course, is just to help you broaden your picture of the nursing mother a bit. The object is not to get you to adopt a whole new self-image, but to loosen up your options so that you can see more about who you are as, among other things, a parent of a nursing baby or child.

Another thing for fathers and mothers to be wary of is pressure from this sex culture's propaganda. It seems that all we hear is that if you do not have intercourse complete with one or more orgasms every so often, whatever your favorite expert's stated or implied interval is, you are doomed to separate bedrooms from now on (or at least to sex therapy or something).

When one partner is uneasy about sex, it is a time to show love in other ways—talk, touch, and be patient. A pause in sexual activity is a physical imperative when the man is having badly confused feelings about sex; it is equally imperative when the woman is similarly confused about sex. Love allows for pauses, even shutdowns in the lovemaking while either partner or both make adjustments, while they talk and mature and think things through.

FEELING USED

One statement so many nursing mothers make at some time or another while our little ones are nursing is that we feel used. We wish there were a time again when we could call our bodies our own. One mother talks about "a lack of privacy— an invasion of self" which carried over for a while to her relationship with her husband. These feelings come when our children want a lot of nursing when we do not feel that we can say no. At the same time our husbands want sexual attention, and we may not feel we can say no to them either. These feelings are so common at one time or another during the time we are nursing that I would almost call them universal.

This is a situation in which feelings about nursing and feelings about sex are interacting. We are lumping the needs of two different people together and letting ourselves get overwhelmed. We are forgetting the third person who also has needs to be expressed—ourselves. If we give up on ourselves with an, "Alas, such is the life of a wife and mother," we are apt to become emotionally walled in so that we cannot enjoy either husband or child.

Instead, it is necessary to dialogue. Discuss your feelings about nursing with your child as best you can, depending on her age. Cut back on nursing a little bit if it helps and if your child can be comfortable with your doing that. Or give your child a chance for a "nursing binge" for a few days to see whether you can sate him and thereby reduce his demands on you after a few days.

Discuss your feelings with your husband, too. He is the person who can aid you most. Do not use your discussion time to complain about how demanding your child is, how much he nurses, and so on. The response you will most likely get to such complaining is pressure to wean and/or send the child out to preschool—or both. Nor is that unkind on his part; when you complain that way, it sounds to all the world as if weaning or separation is exactly the kind of relief you are asking for.

Talk about your child's needs and your husband's needs for access to your body. Let your husband know that you feel that loving both him and your child is very important. Tell him what you are doing to reduce your feelings of pressure from your child and fill him in on any progress. Make clear your understanding and sympathy for his frustration when he has to wait because of the needs of the child you are rearing together.

Enlist his support for your need to have the final say over the use of your body. Do not be afraid to ask for some cuddling from him for yourself when you have been babying the baby all day—cuddling without sex if that is the way you need it to be. Learn to say no to sex when you need to (but learn to say no with lots of love). Your life of love with your whole family will be much better in the long run if after a hard day of demands from your children, especially the little ones, you know you can fall into the arms of a man who, if you ask, will cradle you and not insist on making more physical demands on you that day. And do not worry that you are asking too much; there should be plenty of chances for you to do the same thing for him. Besides, for many of us there is sometimes no stronger aphrodisiac than being given love by a man who is not expecting to make love.

THROWING OUT THE STEREOTYPES

One thing that gives us a lot of trouble is a fixed view of what healthy sexual behavior is supposed to be. Whenever our feelings and behavior do not fit the stereotype we become worried that we are not normal, especially these days if we deviate on the side of being less interested in sex. But sexual feelings are like other feelings: They change and grow, and rest; sometimes they get to be too much for us, while other times we think they are gone altogether. There are many ups and downs along with subtle changes and shadings in how we relate as a couple at the dinner table. Why should we expect any less fluctuation in our relationship in bed? Being parents of a nursing baby is just one of the many happenings in life which will reflect themselves in our sexual feelings. Whatever our feelings are now, it is nearly certain that they will have changed in some way or other by a year from now.

RE-STAGING THE LOVEMAKING

There are, of course, practical considerations about sexual fun when you are parents of a nursing toddler—such as what to do if your little one spends most of the night in your bed. The parents' bed (renamed nicely by Tine Thevenin in her book *The Family Bed*) is a good place for little children, as attested to by the fact that so many of them express a need to sleep there. The question is how to make love in a double bed without waking a three-year-old. Most couples do not even try; they leave the child in bed and make love somewhere else. Or they expand the bed space by buying bigger beds, getting more beds, adding mats on the floor.

I find it hard to understand the reasoning of those who

warn that it can somehow damage a child if he should awaken and see you making love. From mankind's beginnings most people have been reared in dwellings with a single sleeping area. Simple reason says that it is a very small minority of the world's babies and children who have reached maturity without the opportunity to awaken while adults were engaged in intercourse. The only reason that interrupting parents happily involved in such a natural activity as lovemaking could be harmful in any way to a little child, it seems to me, stems from our own social rules. Most adults in our society would be absolutely scandalized should he decide to tell the neighbors or try to demonstrate in his childish way with his cousin. We should for this reason protect children over two years of age or so from our own attitudes by making love when they are soundly asleep or in another room. By school age, children are initiated already into our culture and therefore aware of what they are and are not "supposed" to see. They would no doubt find it quite embarrassing to see you enjoying sex.

Living with the younger ones, my wife-and-mother feeling is that as long as neither you nor your baby or young toddler are having uneasy feelings because of being in the same room while you are making love, you only have to have enough distance between the two of you and the child to keep you from disturbing his sleep and to keep his presence from disturbing you.

CHANGES IN BREAST SENSITIVITY

Quite a number of nursing mothers report a considerable reduction in receptiveness to breast stimulation in sex play during the months or years they are nursing. Such a change in feelings is normal, though not universal, and there is nothing to be done to alter it. It is a change which challenges us to find the ways to enjoy sex that please us most under these circumstances. You may say wistfully that breast stimulation used to be really exciting; well, it will be again. Meanwhile you can have fun finding other ways to enjoy each other.

It may be that the various kinds of breast sensations different ones of us experience from nursing and from sex play during the nursing years—sexual excitement from nursing, or lessened interest in breast stimulation in sex play—may result from factors which are as much mental as physical. Our feelings probably grow from the kind of adaptations our individual psychological machinery makes to the business of being a nursing mother. If such is the case, we have no direct control over this adaptation, which occurs without our thinking about it. There is no reason to believe that having either sensitive breasts or not-so-sensitive breasts (or anything in between) is one better than the other. Each is a circumstance to accept and enjoy, for there are advantages either way.

NURSING PADS AND OLD LACE

One final suggestion that I have for nursing mothers comes from patient and supportive "nursing fathers." Please be conscious of how little glamour there is in many nursing bras—not all of them by any means; some of them are pretty. Still, at some time, probably quite a while before your little one weans, you can return to fashion bras, especially those stretchy ones that you can pull up for nursing, or no bra if that is your style. You must still be cautious that any bra you wear fits well, not too tightly. Be alert, too, when you first try a new bra or no bra. Go back to what you have been wearing at the first sign of any breast soreness, and try again in a few weeks. As long as you are comfortable and not afflicted with plugged ducts or breast infections caused by a poorly fitting bra (and as soon as you are able to go without nursing pads which are cumbersome in a fashion bra), your husband will probably be really glad to see the nursing bras go.

FATIGUE AND SEXUALITY

According to Gregory White, MD, the number one enemy of sexuality—greater than anything discussed in this chapter—is excess fatigue, a statement which leads conveniently into the next chapter.

CHAPTER 7

Getting Enough Rest

NIGHT DUTY

As I write this tonight I am sitting in bed with my youngest asleep beside me threatening to wake up any minute. So I know full well that this sleeping business is no joke. Our adult lifestyle and children's ever-changing sleep patterns seem to interfere with each other repeatedly. Just as you get everything worked out, your child changes again.

First of all, nursing is not the cause of your losing sleep. That is hard to believe when the whole household is quietly asleep—that is everyone but you. The little one nods off, still clinging to your nipple, but like so many mothers who slept well while their small infants were nursing, you now find it difficult to sleep while nursing a little child. So you, little one attached, lie grudgingly awake in the peaceful night. Every time you remove your nipple from his mouth, no matter how carefully, he starts kicking and crying. Under these circumstances you are not likely to be very receptive to my suggestion that it is not the nursing that is keeping you awake.

Well, technically, you are awake because of the nursing. But I would suggest that in reality you are awake because of being the mother of your child at this time in her life. I would suggest that if you were not lying there half-awake nursing, you would probably be stumbling around fixing a bottle or an apple slice, or rocking and patting, or fumbling among the toys under the bed looking for a lost pacifier. It has been my experience that, even though I too have at times felt really resentful of night nursings, they never disrupted my sleep as badly as did tending to the nighttime needs of my toddler who did not nurse.

The best times for me nursing at night were when I discovered the warm, quiet of the night and the security of lying close between two people who loved me. The worst times were when I wrestled with my own private nighttime demons and felt suffocated between the same bodies that made me feel secure the night before. The nursing situations were of course the same both times; the difference was what was going on in my head.

WHEN NEEDS CLASH

Caring for our children at night presents a situation in which our needs seem to be in direct conflict with theirs. Most of us become quite childlike ourselves when we go to sleep, so it often feels as if we are being asked to care for a little person when we are not so big ourselves right then. And so often we carry an irrational resentment of the night's interrupted sleep into the day. Some days we have big plans and are, of course, disappointed that we are draggy because of lost sleep. Most days, though, we merely need to slow down our pace to cope with being sleepy. Sleepiness is one of life's many normal conditions that we can cope with very well if we do not fight it or push ourselves beyond what sleepy people can do.

Our initial, immature—100% understandable—reaction to interrupted sleep is to lash out at the child, to try to make him pay attention to our needs, too. Of course, when we do this (and most all of us do some time in one way or another), we communicate little and generally end up losing even more sleep. Many parent-hours of hard experience tell us that it is much more productive to apply adult heads to modifying living patterns so that children get the care they need twenty-four hours a day while adults get enough rest most of the time.

Night is a scary time for people—not just little people

either. The nights of the first few years are the nights which will teach our children how to cope with the fears that come with darkness. The very best source of comfort at night is the presence of another person, or other people. You can teach your child to sleep alone if that is important enough to you that you want to put out all the effort outlined in many standard books of child care and if you find it necessary to let your child risk nightmares and such. As a parent you have to get extra rest in the day, too, to help minimize the physical drain on you from this arrangement, for you will need to get up and present yourself bodily at your child's bedside from time to time during her growing-up years in an effort to prove to her that this sleeping arrangement is indeed safe and that you are still available when needed. You may have to do this several times a night or several times a year depending on your child, for a child must not be left alone at night if she is frightened. It may also be necessary to provide a regular bedtime ritual and a cuddly object, both of which will help ward off the fears of the night.

You can on the other hand choose to teach your child to seek security in the night by getting close to people. Looking at mankind as a whole, it is clear that sleeping near other people surely has survival value. It is easier to keep warm and to defend ourselves from real dangers in the night if we are near other people. Only in a society in which we can burn fuel freely to heat large homes, and only where the danger of predators—human or animal—is very low would we dare put a baby or small child in a room separate from his parents.

I must be quick to add, though, that my bias toward teaching kids to seek company when they are scared at night began with nothing at all so lofty as a desire to help them be well-adjusted about nighttime or to protect them from dangers in the night. I have been guided solely by laziness and distaste for lost sleep.

One way to increase your rest at night is to nurse at night and to do it in bed (though some do prefer to doze in a comfortable chair). Doing this is ever so much more restful than sitting on the edge of a frightened child's bed until the alligators go away.

Another way to get more rest is to be flexible about sleeping arrangements. Your family may sleep best with Junior between you, or at your side.

Learning to offer both breasts from the same side so that

you don't have to roll over may help reduce interruption in your sleep and can enable you to keep your child in the safest or most comfortable part of the bed.

You may need to put your bed against the wall or your mattress on the floor for a while so you do not have to worry about his falling off. Or if he is wriggly and you keep each other awake, you may want to fasten a crib, with the side dropped, securely to the side of your bed. That way you can roll him in and out of it easily. A mat, sleeping bag, or mattress for your baby or child on the floor near your bed may be your best bet.

It may even be that it will be more comfortable for you to have your child in another room for one reason or another. We moved one of our children out of our room while he was still a baby because he snored so loudly. Another family found it best to put their child in her own room for at least part of the night "since every sound woke her, including deep breaths and dropped socks." You may want to try putting your older baby or toddler in bed with an older sibling if there is one. Consider a bed or mattress on the floor or a recliner in his room where you can nurse in complete comfort, or where daddy or big brother can cuddle with the little one when that works out.

Night waking may become less wakeful for you if you provide your walking child with a place of his own to sleep that he can get out of easily at night, like a low bed or mattress rather than a crib, so that he can come to you when he needs to. Most parents are glad not to have to get up at night while still caring for their children who do awaken and need them.

Whatever you do, make sure you provide secure feelings for your children at night; and make sure you do it in the least sleep-disturbing way possible for your family. Also be prepared to change from one easy approach to a different easy approach as you notice things becoming different. Your child is growing and changing fast, and no one else in the family can be expected to stay the same forever either. So be adaptable. And be prepared to help with nighttime fears as long as your children live with you. School age children are grateful to know that after a nightmare there is a place near you where they can come quietly to sleep with a feeling of your protection, or to know that you will come sleep near them.

FREQUENT NIGHT NURSING

It helps your child and therefore helps you to get more sleep at night if you do a few obvious things which can enable your child to sleep better. One is helping her to keep cool enough or warm enough. On hot nights it may be necessary to use air conditioning a bit more than usual to help a restless little one sleep. (Many of us are finding how comfortable it can be for a child to have an electric fan hung high out of reach for such nights, and it is much less expensive than air conditioning.)

On cold nights pajamas on a baby or toddler are helpful for those who will wear them, even if no one else in the house bothers with night clothes. Children are usually near four before they can sleep without kicking their covers off. So one way to avoid being awakened by a shivering tot is to cover him all up with warm sleepers—the kind with feet. Double diapers and plastic pants help a lot, too, because wet bedding and pajamas can make him even colder. (You will find nursing in a cold room when your shoulders have to stick out of the covers a less chilling experience for you if you wear a long-sleeved pajama top or robe. A loose-fitting pullover works fine; a nightshirt or robe that opens in the front is even more convenient for easy, warm nighttime nursing.)

Once in a while it is hunger that causes a child to wake frequently at night. If you suspect this might be so, offer your child a filling snack (like a banana, a peanut butter sandwich, something good left over from supper, an egg, etc.) before she gets really sleepy and before she brushes her teeth. It is fine for her to take a crunchy snack like raw carrot, celery, apple, cabbage, etc., to bed with her. You will probably have to offer several things to be sure whether or not she is hungry. You may also want to try the same thing in the middle of the night. The limit under starlight of your culinary genius may well be cutting slices of apple. But, if it turns out that your growing child does sleep better with a 2 A.M. snack for a while, you can start preparing during the day to be sure you have something ready and easy to grab at night.

Some children, quite the opposite, seem to be disturbed by rumblings in their tummies if they eat at bedtime. They sleep better if they do their eating earlier in the evening.

There are health problems that can cause night waking too. Some children are troubled by stuffy noses at night— when they have a cold, or because of allergies. Your child is much less likely to be allergic than is a bottle-fed one, but some breastfed babies still do grow up into children with allergic sniffles. These children will sleep better if they are kept away from whatever substance it is that bothers them. Wool blankets or feather pillows top the list of things that can cause nighttime sniffles. Be sure to consult your doctor if a stuffy nose stays around for a long time and disrupts your child's sleep. She will be able to help you identify the cause of the congestion and advise you in making your child (and thereby your whole family) more comfortable at night.

The onset of a cold or teething may reveal themselves in restlessness at night even before other symptoms appear. So many of us have resisted our children's waking at night "for no reason" only to find later that such a problem was just beginning. How cold and hardhearted we felt looking back!

Other possibilities to check with your doctor when your child seems unusually restless at night include pinworms, earache, and constipation.

Mosquito bites can awaken little people (and big people too). It is wise to keep on hand whatever medication you find most helpful for itchy bites. In addition, after an active day children often experience leg aches which can make it hard to go to sleep or can wake them up. Gentle massage and an extra cover usually relieve this discomfort.

Many children wake up while they are urinating or immediately afterwards. This can happen in any child, but is quite common in toddlers who are being toilet trained too early and too vigorously. Relaxing any efforts toward toilet training can lead to a gradual reduction in waking for this reason.

With the whole list of physical causes of waking mother often at night out of the way, still the majority of you with questions about this matter are reading on, because physical factors do not seem to be involved in night waking most of the time. The reason that most children wake up at night is their normal, immature sleep pattern which will be changed only by the passage of time. I like to discuss the physical factors first, though, because by the time you have checked them all out, your child may have outgrown this up-and-down-all-night time all by himself, and thus we have an opportunity to take bows for effecting such a marvelous "cure."

One fruitful place to look for reasons for restlessness in the night is tensions in the day. The things we need to look at are not so much things that make us tense, though our tensions cannot be ignored completely, but the things which make our children tense. Each child tolerates experiences differently, each in his own way, and on his own timetable. An increase in our activities, especially activities which consume our attention or take us away from our children can result in our children's having more uneasy feelings during the day and an increase in restlessness at night.

An overtired mother can also make a child tense and unhappy so that he is up more frequently at night. This situation can become a vicious circle, so it is wise when you see this happening to employ some of the "survival techniques" discussed later in this chapter in order to get more rest and break the cycle.

I do not want any of you who are living with a child who is wakeful at night to take on guilt, thinking that you must be an awful mother to allow "tensions" into your child's life. He needs to learn to deal with the small, everyday situations which leave him tense, and he does this very effectively when he seeks the comfort of being near you and nursing—during the day and at night. He is learning to seek comfort by being near his most loved person. He gets into the warm, familiar nursing situation and lets himself feel good again. You are doing your part for his well-being in turn when you make it easy for him to do this. But it may indeed make you tired.

Mothers who work away from home especially notice their children's need for nursing at night. Many working moms, even though they are really tired, tell me that they appreciate the closeness and softening of anxieties that night nursings provide for both mother and child. Frequent nursing at night can be essential for toddlers whose mothers are away during the day.

Children vary so much in what makes them anxious that it is impossible for one mother to analyze another mother's activities and say for certain that this or that is why her child is up several times at night. The mother whose little one sleeps all night is not thereby proved to be a "better mother"; to begin with she probably has one of those children who just are not wakeful.

Some children seem to adapt easily to new situations. Others are so disoriented in their early years that they must have almost every minute of love and attention a full-time mother can give and still are restless at night. Nothing you can do will make the very tense child become a completely easygoing one. You can make some difference, though, in how much tension your child takes to bed at night by gentling her days.

I would urge any mother who is walking around bleary-eyed because of being awake nursing so much at night to simplify the daytime, avoiding situations which make the child clingy (or wildly overactive—a kind of behavior that can signal the same threatened feelings in a child as does shy clinging). New people, new places, new activities, projects that occupy parents' or even siblings' attention for longer blocks of time than usual, activities that increase the separation of mother and child or father and child—all these are possible sources of tension for your child.

Different children enjoy different kinds of challenges in their daily lives, so it is impossible to draw up a checklist that says, "Do these things every day," and, "Never do these things." You can judge best by watching your own child's behavior. Watch for unusual signals of stress (one of my children avoids threatening situations by going to sleep), and sometimes you will be able to spot a situation that is just too much for your child right now.

There is one kind of tension that you would not want to eliminate if you could, however, and that is the one that results from your own child's eagerness to tackle new things. When your child wants to learn to walk, to talk with people outside the immediate family, to step on a bug, to tie his own shoes, to toilet train, to go to school, and on and on through the ambitions any young child may have—when your child pushes himself to accomplish more, he is going to experience some increase in his level of anxiety and require some babying to help him handle it. The lady who some years ago trained so many of us in the Southwestern U.S.A. for work in La Leche League describes this pattern of self-imposed tension and comfort-seeking as the "Yo-Yo Theory." The farther they venture away on their quest for independence, the closer they need to come back into baby things to make sure everything is okay. Both the venturing out and the coming back are necessary for growing up and away. And, like a yo-yo, they do gradually come back less and less urgently.

SURVIVING WHEN NIGHT NURSINGS ARE NECESSARY

The key to surviving the active, unpredictable preschool years is laziness—well, laziness coupled with the ability to accept tiredness as a part of life sometimes. I know that what you do just to keep your toddler from dumping the laundry soap into the aquarium or from burning the encyclopedias in the fireplace is far from laziness. But most of us have visions of shiny floors (*sans* any "yellow wax build-up"), kitchens that smell as clean as they look, and a germ-free bathroom bowl. If we do not meet the standards set by our mothers (or mothers-in-law) and those TV commercial housewives, we feel inadequate and lazy. Well, in my opinion, if you are enjoying your time with your child and are having a happy give and take between what he wants to do and what you want to do, you are far from inadequate. If the day does not leave you time or energy to make the beds, then you may feel that you have been lazy. You have not been lazy at all really; but if you are like me, it will be easier just to say that you have been than to try to explain.

The most helpful lazy thing to do when you have lost sleep at night is to lie down during the day. You can usually find some time when you can lie down and nurse your little one to sleep. That is an excellent opportunity for rest for both of you. When you are being awakened at night, do not use your child's naptime to catch up on undone work that you are feeling guilty about. I repeat myself perhaps, but only because it is important and because we women are hardheaded about learning to take care of ourselves—be lazy. Lie beside your child and enjoy the warm, quiet time. Or drift off to sleep. He will help you dump that fizzy stuff in the toilet bowl later, or tomorrow. You will get done what you have to get done. I have learned from experience, no matter what "they" say, that a refrigerator is no harder to clean after eight months than after one. So do not worry about it. These things can wait when they have to.

If you reach a time when you are frequently exhausted while your little one is going strong, or a time when you need a nap but he does not, it is time to set up a safe, fun, locked room in which you can lie down and doze without fear of your child's hurting himself or you. You need to install a lock your child cannot operate—perhaps one high on the inside of the door. The room needs to contain interesting books and toys—things your child likes—things which will not hurt you if he drops them on your head while you are asleep. Electrical outlets need safety covers, and things plugged into outlets (like clocks) need to be plugged in behind heavy furniture. There should be no appliances in the room for her to practice operating, no plastic bags, medicines, cleaning supplies—nothing dangerous. Nor should there be anything fragile or valuable enough for you to have to worry about.

It may be best for the "child-proof" room to be a playroom or child's bedroom, or your may prefer to fix your own bedroom to be safe for you and your child. This room is a place to which you can go, where you can lie down, relax your vigil over your child's inquisitiveness a bit, even fall asleep if your little one gets occupied with something in the room for a while. Even just lying down while he nurses, pries your eyelids open, flicks your fingernails, and all the other ways a child is likely to use your body for entertainment—just lying down is more refreshing than you might expect. When she is bored with nursing, roll over on your stomach, and she will probably give you what one mother described as a "poor man's massage" by climbing all over you.

Another source of relief for you when you are up a great deal at night is another person with whom your child is comfortable. Perhaps daddy will entertain the little one for a while in the evening so you can get a nap or a leisurely bath. Some mothers go to bed early with the child for a while; usually doing this includes an understanding with their mates that they can wake their wives sometime later in the evening for conversation and whatever else may develop. Another great help can be a responsible older child—your own, or a neighbor's—who is willing to play with your little one while you nap. Since you are right there in the house, even a sharp seven-year-old can fill the bill (and a child this age may not even demand the going rate for baby sitters).

By all means, be ingenious and clever. There are ways to survive without making anyone have to do without what she—or he—needs.

EXPENDABLE NIGHTTIME NURSINGS

Many children need a lot of attention at night well into childhood. Many others drop one and then another nighttime nursing over the months or years just by beginning to sleep longer stretches. Now and then it is possible to hurry up the progress toward longer stretches of sleep a little bit—not much, though—by gently avoiding nursing when you sense that your child is very sleepy and not really intent upon nursing. You can roll on your stomach and see whether your child's halfhearted whimpering and pummeling fades back into the steady breathing of sleep, or if it becomes more urgent. Or you can have daddy or an older sibling pat or rock him back to sleep. If you have guessed wrong and your child is feeling a strong need to nurse, there is no harm done. He is quite able to make it clear to you what he needs and will not hesitate to do so.

What I have not suggested for eliminating nighttime waking and nursing is the "letting him cry it out" approach. Letting a child cry can be effective in teaching him not to wake his parents, but often at the expense of his ever being able to feel safe at night. You may pretend to be fast asleep on your stomach while you make sure the child beside you is really awake and needing to nurse. Or you may snooze while one of your "reinforcements" tries to get him back to sleep. In either case you are doing quite a different thing from deserting him in a room by himself (at least as he sees it) to "cry it out." Instead there is a person with him to help him relax back into sleep, or to respond if he tells you that nothing can substitute for nursing this time.

Caring for anxious, wakeful children at night can be tiresome, and we all resent it sometimes. But a combination of flexibility and creative laziness helps us to survive these nights and the days that follow them. Keeping our children secure and comfortable at night is a contribution toward a lifetime of easy sleep for them, an objective worthy of the weariness we may feel now. Hang in there; these nighttime needs will not stay so urgent forever.

THE "NO NURSING UNTIL DAYLIGHT" CONTRACT

A few very verbal children are able to make an agreement with their mothers not to ask to nurse until it gets to be light outside. Then they pounce eagerly, ready for a long early morning cuddle-and-nurse.

Most mothers who suggest such an agreement meet either protests or blank stares from their youngsters. But an occasional child finds the idea acceptable, and mother gets a little more sleep as a result. A small added bonus is the comic glee with which he flies into mother's arms, usually at the first glimmer of daylight.

An interesting corollary of this arrangement is the "No Nursing Until Dark" Contract. Once in a while a mother has been able to reduce pressure upon herself from people around her by persuading her child to nurse only in the evening and during the night.

As long as the child is comfortable and is not showing signs of distress in other ways, there should be no problem with an agreement of this type. Do keep in mind, though, that a preschool child is not mature enough yet to make long-range plans about something so compelling as nursing. The agreement may be fine for a while, but when she reaches another stage in her growing, or a rough spot, the contract may need to come up for renegotiation.

LONG BEDTIME NURSINGS

So often we take a cranky tot to bed and lie down to nurse him to sleep—and lie there, and lie there. . . . Sometimes it makes us really angry to be "trapped" when we would so much prefer to be involved in adult activities during the evening.

Many families, I must be quick to say, are comfortable with a long nursing at the child's bedtime. This is certainly a very peaceful way for your child to drift off to sleep. Some mothers take a nap at this time and find themselves refreshed for the late evening grown-up world. On occasion the child even puts mom to sleep instead of the other way around. In a delightful little family comedy it can be the child who reappears in the living room and then helps dad tease mom about who was putting whom to bed. At any rate, with or without comedy, if you are happy with these nursings, by all means do not interfere with something that is working for you.

If you have not achieved positive feelings, especially about nursing so long at bedtime, there are a number of options you may want to consider. First of all, is your child sleepy? Is your child who is so hard to get to sleep waking up very early in the morning or waking often at night? Preschool children require less sleep than most people wishfully may think. Crabby, "sleepy" behavior in the evening can result from many things besides sleepiness: The first thing that comes to mind is that we adults are tired and start our own activities (or inactivities) that do not include our little ones. We may be less mobile and less interesting than during the day. Your child may like it better when you are sorting laundry and talking to her than when you are watching TV or writing letters. Another thing—our children, like us, may get tired and a bit irritable quite a while before they are ready to fall asleep. Sometimes they nurse a while, doze a bit, and then are (horrors!) their perky selves for another hour or so—just the way we adults do sometimes in the evening.

One approach to problems in the evening is to forget about bedtimes with preschoolers. School-aged children are into our scheduled world and have to adhere to some sort of bedtime; besides, they seem to need more sleep than do the younger ones. The little ones, however, can drop off to sleep whenever they are ready—tiny ones prone on daddy's knees or bigger ones sitting beside daddy, or in mommy's arms after nursing off and on throughout the evening, or on the beanbag chair in front of the TV, or wherever they curl up and conk out. As hallowed as the children's bedtime is in our motherhood lore, it is in practice many times a source of friction that is just as well done away with—for the little children at any rate.

The possible drawback of forgetting bedtimes is the fact that, in many families, the adults will have little people for company most of the evening. It is possible, though few believe it any more, to have enjoyable evenings with children around. Sometimes in a family of several children, after the school kids are in bed is the only time daddy gets to enjoy the youngest without competition from other children. And sometimes it is possible to trade evening cocktails alone for breakfast alone for a few months or years. Some couples, however, may find that their time in the evening is irreplaceable; and of course in these households it is wise to help the children get to sleep—at least a little while before the adults' bedtime. This may mean learning to enjoy a long nursing.

It could give you a kind of closed-in feeling, too, if you find that you cannot go out in the evenings because your child

I've just talked to God and he says I can have more nee-nee.

gets cranky and needs to nurse to sleep and really needs to do
it at home in bed. Yet there are several constructive courses
you can take. First, you can just wait. Your child will outgrow
the time of having to nurse to fall asleep if you are not there.
Most children at a fairly young age, as long as they are happy
with their caretaker, especially daddy, learn to fall asleep with
rocking or walking, or just sitting with him as he reads or
watches TV. A leisurely bath and reading a story can help.

Many children do not want to go to bed without nursing,
but most will fall asleep as long as they can stay close to daddy
or a familiar sitter. If your child is not yet comfortable with
falling asleep in anyone's arms but yours, be patient. It will
probably not be long before she is.

Another way to deal with the need to nurse at bedtime (or
with the toddler who stays up very late) is to rearrange your
plans to fit her schedule. There are many places—visiting
friends or eating out for instance—that you can take your
wide-awake child. If your child, on the other hand, needs you
to be there for an early bedtime nursing, you can arrange to go
out or to entertain after he is asleep. Either way the adjustments you are making are not permanent changes in your

social life. They are temporary changes you are making to make life easier. Besides, changes give you an opportunity to toy with different lifestyles. What is a cocktail party like with a two-year-old among the guests? What about a leisurely dinner well after 8:00 at a gourmet restaurant—or at Taco Tico for that matter? The possibilities are endless if you have imagination; and without your child's bedtime needs you might never have thought of them. As for the things you cannot do now, you will be able to do them again. The time during which your little one will need you so much in the evening is far short of forever. In fact it is hardly a moment in the space of your lifetime.

The way many families—mine included—have dealt with the problem of having mom feeling trapped at the bedtime nursing is to have dad take over the bedtime routine with the youngest. Freeing mothers like me who are impatient with bedtime nursings is not the only reason, though, that families use this sort of routine. Many fathers enjoy this special cuddly time and responsibility in the care of their little children.

This sort of arrangement can begin in infancy when dad holds the baby in the evenings until she wants to nurse. Mom nurses and then returns her to daddy and so on back and forth until the baby is sound asleep. Gradually there gets to be less nursing and more cuddling with daddy until the day when falling asleep goes more smoothly if you are conveniently "busy" in another part of the house for as long as she is happy with her father.

This type of routine for helping a child fall asleep is not as popular as having mother nurse the child to sleep, but it is certainly a good option for those families who enjoy it. Having dad help the youngest fall asleep can be especially helpful when you have other children with bedtime needs, too.

There is a wide range of options in the framework of trying to balance the parents' needs and the children's needs in a way that is comfortable for everybody. There are no rules about when bedtime must be for a little child, or how it must be structured, or by whom, so do feel free to be creative. Adapt when and how you get him to sleep, not to what is acceptable in the neighborhood, but to what works in your family.

CHAPTER 8

Unique Circumstances

WORKING OR STUDYING AWAY FROM YOUR CHILD

If you have a commitment of some sort (a job, classes, etc.) that takes you away from a baby in his first year, the mechanics of nursing can be rather difficult. One mother whose friends, like so many people, could not see how she could possibly nurse a baby while she was working, responded, "Oh, I don't. I wait until I get home." But of course there is more than that to nursing and working in the early months.

Once you have weathered the special problems of maintaining your milk supply through your child's babyhood, or if you have waited until your child is past infancy to go out to work, school, or whatever, (or an increasingly available third alternative, if you have kept your baby with you at your job or classes until she became just too inquisitive and mobile to be safe or accepted there)—in any of these circumstances nursing should no longer present difficulties different from what any mother of a child the age of yours may have to deal with. It is mothering your child that will challenge you.

I realize that it is taboo these days to talk about the fact that children are able to grow up with less anxiety and therefore have the very best opportunity for full physical and mental development if they are able to be with their mothers, especially during the first three years. Talking about the disadvantages of mother-baby or mother-toddler separation is supposed to inflict guilt feelings upon mothers who must be away from their little ones—just as mentioning the disadvantages of formula feeding was until recently supposed to make mothers who do not breastfeed suffer from remorse.

It seems to me that the mother who faces such an extremely rare problem that she cannot breastfeed is not the one who is going to feel guilty. Nor is the mother in the not-nearly-so-rare circumstance these days, sad to say, in which she must be away from her young child, going to experience true guilt—disappointment and regret perhaps, but not guilt. For these mothers are facing what all of us have to deal with at some time or another, that is, rearing children as best we can under less-than-ideal circumstances. The mother who has to be away from her child regularly can, as can any mother who must live in an imperfect world, do the very best for her child that the realities of life will permit her to do.

It is when we voluntarily create a way of life that is not as good for our children as it should be that true guilt feelings surface, and rightly so. And it may well be that when a mother chooses to be away from a child too young to function well in her absence that the long-range ill effects of premature separation are most likely to occur. For one thing, children may be able to perceive very early through their mothers' behavior that a necessary deprivation is one thing and that being deliberately shortchanged is quite another. Also, even under circumstances that make separation necessary for too long and too soon in the child's life, a mother who is doing her best for her child and knows it should be able to feel good about herself and be in the best possible frame of mind to overcome the kinds of problems that she may see arising as a result of regular separation from her child. "Your working in itself will not ruin your children," says Alice Skelsey, "but it does add one more factor to the interactions in all your family relationships. You have to interpret accurately the effects of that factor."

A mother on the other hand who does have reasonable alternatives (such as taking a loan or a job at home, being content with a lower standard of living, etc.) by which she could avoid separation is more subject to being handicapped in her mothering by feelings of guilt. And guilt feelings tend to compound any difficulties resulting from separation by interfering with a mother's ability to care for her child in ways that are both sensitive and sensible.

It is on the subject of voluntary separation of mothers and very young children that much of what we read these days is so misleading. In a laudable attempt to overcome stereotypes of what we women must do with our lives, many writers have gone too far. They have undermined much of the support system for those of us who prefer to take primary responsibility for our children (Cardozo). And worse still, people these days have become much too casual in suggesting that families can do just as well using temporary mother-substitutes as with the real mother—just as a few years ago people were so certain that formula was just as good as mother's milk for babies. The truth is that, just as mother's milk cannot be duplicated, neither can mother herself.

John Bowlby early in his career suggested "that the young child's hunger for his mother's love and presence is as great as his hunger for food and that in consequence her absence inevitably generates a powerful sense of loss and anger," and his continuing research has served to confirm the validity of this early assertion.

Pediatricians, too, are urging mothers more often these days to keep their children out of day-care centers because of repeated infections due to too-frequent exposure to large groups of children from other families (Pediatric News).

Some sensitive women who do their best to serve not just as baby sitters but as mother substitutes for babies and preschoolers are distressed to find themselves experiencing moments of love and intimacy which they feel belong only to the child's parents. "She wouldn't want me to share such a special smile or moment with her husband," one woman said. "I don't know how she can let me have these moments with her child. She is missing so much."

Separation in the early years can have profound significance for both child and mother and should not be undertaken or recommended except under the most urgent of circumstances. When separation from a baby or toddler is unavoidable, though, there are ways to reduce the feelings of loss and anger that Dr. Bowlby mentions.

First of all you will want to minimize your separation. Delay the separation for as long as possible, and then be away for as few hours as you can manage. Try to have your child as close as possible to where you will be so that you might be able to have lunch or maybe a break together. If you have a long drive morning and evening, then you and your little one will enjoy it more if you are together during that time.

The greatest risk in any family to our mothering of a preschool child is that we try to do too much besides working alongside, playing with, and listening to the child. This applies to all of us, whether we spend time away from him or not. A child in the second and third year needs a great deal of attention. These busy years of rapid growth are times when we all have to minimize our other commitments in order to help our children grow.

If you find that you must be away from your child regularly, then with most children most of the time your outside job will need to be your only commitment besides being mommy. You may on occasion find time to do other things, but you are wise not to make promises or to count on time for other projects, and that may include much of the housework.

Even finding time for yourself alone may be out of the question some days. As tempting as it may be to try to get your young toddler to nap for a while when you come home or to go to bed early, it is more important to the future happiness and security of your child—and therefore to the happiness and security of you and your family—that you try to be available to him as much as you can. If, for example, you need to lie down, perhaps you and your child can lie down together. Or maybe he'd like to join you while you unwind in a hot bath. You can figure out things to calm yourself down and shift gears from the workaday world to your mother-and-homemaker world without shutting him out.

One of the most troublesome errors that we women make when we take on responsibilities away from home is that we try to add this job to the one we already have at home. So many women try to work an eight-hour day and then come home to do all the cooking, cleaning, and laundry. Few of us have that much energy to give. If we add a two-year-old to the picture, the situation becomes impossible.

Many children whose mothers spend several hours away from them daily wake several times at night for contact with mother and perhaps for nursing. Mothers who undertake two careers, mothering and the other one they have, need to appreciate how essential these nighttime get-togethers are. A baby or toddler who is away from her mother daily usually needs to be able to spend the night in her parents' bed.

Being awake at night with your child, however, or even partially awake, is going to put a strain on you unless you can go to bed earlier for a while or get extra rest some other way. The possibility of night duty as part of your mothering career is one of many reasons that you must take extra care of yourself and not require yourself to do much of what you have done in the past. (Actually no mother of a child in the second or third year should expect to accomplish great things beyond rearing a great kid.) You should expect to need a lot of help with household tasks, or just to let as many as possible of them go.

There is only so much time and energy available to you, and you need to set your priorities and work from the top down. On those days when your husband has collected a whole load of laundry from under the furniture and supper is leftovers heating in the oven, you should not allow yourself to feel bad about the housework. Your child needs your attention much more than he needs a clean house or gourmet meals. He cares nothing about whether his clothes are neatly folded or fished out of a basket of clothes washed day-before-yesterday. But having you frenzied and worn out would bother him a lot. So keep first things first.

No doubt what you can get done will change from time to time. There are times for a mother who works away from her child, as for everyone, when the child enjoys helping around the house, when life is easy, when he sleeps well at night. Then mother and the little one can spend their time together on whatever tasks seem important, be it cleaning, sewing, or visiting museums. At other times, the child cannot spare mother's attention for a moment, and then the family has to make whatever adjustments are necessary to function while mother is occupied exclusively with her two careers. Sometimes it becomes obvious that this child's need for mother is so great because of a crisis or illness, or just because of his temperament, that he cannot spare her for the other career. Then it is necessary to seek ways to suspend not only the housework but the other career as well.

Nursing a preschooler when you are working away from him is not difficult. In fact, it is a great pleasure, a warm and intense greeting between mother and child after separation. The difficulties for a mother with another career have to do with adapting herself both to the rigidity of the adult world and the flexibility needed to care for a rapidly growing and changing little child. Many mothers who are away from their children appreciate nursing greatly and use it to help maintain the intimacy and close communication with their little ones that are essential in building a warm and healthy family now and in the future. But even nursing cannot guarantee complete security for a baby or very young child against the risks of separation from mother. So nursing mothers, like all mothers, must give very careful thought to any decision to undertake a regular, frequent commitment away from a very young child.

TWINS

Mothers who are nursing twins experience very much the same joys and difficulties as their little ones become older as do mothers nursing one. It is true that those times when both need to nurse at once, sometimes rather awkward with babies who need to be lifted and held to the breast, become easier when they are toddlers able to climb into mother's lap and position themselves. Also, nursing as long as each child needs to nurse may have special value with these children in that twins tend to find themselves blended together in people's minds and grow weary of being treated as one being. Nursing can be a private individual time for each child, at least sometimes. Natural weaning can give each child the opportunity to express her own needs and have them met one-to-one.

Sometimes twins will wean at about the same time. Sometimes one will be through with nursing long before the other. They do not necessarily wean as a unit any more than they breathe as a unit. Like any other situation in which you might be nursing siblings, you should regard your nursing relationship with each as unique and not much influenced by the other child's nursing.

YOUR ADOPTED CHILD

If natural weaning makes good sense for life with "homemade" children, it seems doubly reasonable for the mother who has made the extra effort often involved in beginning to nurse her adopted baby. In fact ever so many mothers who have had to overcome challenges of any sort in getting started at nursing are, not surprisingly, quite reluctant to give up nursing before they have to.

While many adoptive mothers do establish a full milk supply for the baby's first six months or so, many do not. If you should be one of those who does not have the experience of being able to nurse completely without supplementation, the nursing time after nine months or one year (or maybe even sooner) can be a special pleasure, for at last nursing for you and your baby is completely natural. Like other children this age, your child will eat whatever he needs from the table and come to you for your comfort and your milk when that is what he needs. Your special efforts have been rewarded; even if not at first, now for sure you can meet nursing needs completely for that child who, as the anonymous poem reads, grew not under your heart, but in it.

YOUR LAST CHILD

There is much written about a family's tendency to indulge the last child, to enjoy his immaturity, and to allow him to stay a baby longer than previous children in the family. Of course you should not indulge your child to the point that you deny him plenty of guidance, needed limits, and opportunity for growth. But short of such an extreme you need fear no harm from enjoying your youngest as much as you want to.

Perhaps, as most writers suggest, we sometimes function differently as parents in rearing our last child because of sadness that we will have no one else to baby once this child is grown, but I am not sure. It could be that sometimes the desire to have a baby in the family is one reason that in many families the last child nurses longer than her older siblings.

There is, however, a simpler reason, too obvious perhaps for us to see, that so many of us are more permissive with the youngest child and that he may nurse longer than his older siblings. There are simply fewer factors that interfere with an easy, relaxed approach toward life with the youngest child, and toward his nursing.

By the time the youngest is born, we have experience—

not always a lot, but certainly more than we had the first time. We are much more confident and, therefore, much less easily shaken by the questions or criticisms of others. We know from experience that our children outgrow infantile behaviors, so these behaviors are not threatening to us any more. And, most significantly of all, we do not become pregnant again or have the needs of a still younger child to meet. The circumstances of our lives are sufficient all by themselves to explain why we feel much less urge to hasten the youngest one's growing up. He is likely to nurse longer if he is so inclined just because there is usually less going on to keep him from it.

CHAPTER 9

When Nursing Presents Challenges

NIPPLE DISCOMFORT

Occasionally a mother will remark on a change in how her nipples feel when her child nurses from the way they felt when he was an infant. The older child's nursing is uncomfortable sometimes, and tends to keep her awake at night.

The most likely explanation for the change some mothers notice is the result of a decrease in milk supply coupled with their children's great efficiency in milking the breast. Nursing is comfortable as long as milk is flowing at least a bit. As your little one grows older and nurses less frequently your production of milk decreases eventually to a point at which you no longer manufacture milk quickly enough to keep the sinuses behind your nipple from becoming completely empty when your child nurses for more than a few minutes. Without the lubrication of the flowing milk some mothers find nursing a little bit uncomfortable.

When nursing does not feel good because of no milk flowing, it helps to switch to the other breast if your child is willing (and when half-asleep he may not be). The other breast will have milk, or will have had time to build up a little more if he has already nursed on that side. Either way, switching can relieve the discomfort temporarily—perhaps long enough for him to finish.

Interestingly enough, such nipple discomfort, if you ever experience it at all, will probably not occur every time your child nurses longer than it takes to pretty well drain your breast of milk. You are most likely to feel minor pain when you are, for reasons of your own, impatient for this particular nursing session to be finished. Perhaps you tense yourself in eagerness to get away, or perhaps you focus your attention on the nursing and its sensations. At other times, when you are indifferent to the nursing or enjoying it, there may be no discomfort at all.

It is not uncommon to experience on occasion sore spots where the child's teeth rub (though there are disorders symptomized by blisters which may be confused with soreness from simple friction). Soreness caused by your child's teeth should get better quickly if you consistently air dry your nipples, perhaps sun them a little, and nurse in different positions so that his teeth do not rub the same part of your breast every time. If the soreness persists, have your physician check for other conditions such as cold sores (herpes simplex) or some other infection.

Occasionally after nursing for a year or more, a mother will develop true sore nipples like those which some mothers experience in their babies' first few weeks. If this happens to you, it would be wise to check all the possibilities a brand new mother checks—use of soap or alcohol on nipples, or detergents in your bra or other clothing, a deodorant causing irritation, inadequate air circulation around nipples because of plastic in bra liners or in nursing pads. Careful, brief exposure of your nipples to direct sunlight may help. (See THE WOMANLY ART OF BREASTFEEDING for a more complete discussion of prevention and treatment of sore nipples.)

If, however, none of the measures that are effective in the treatment of red, sore nipples help you, you should consult a physician, preferably one who is comfortable with the idea of nursing beyond babyhood. There are fungi, including those that cause thrush, and skin disorders such as psoriasis, that are occasionally a cause of nipple pain—not often, but occasionally. Early pregnancy can produce nipple tenderness, too. A knowledgeable physician can be a great help in such instances.

MASTITIS

Mastitis or breast infection is a painful inflammation of the breast, usually accompanied by fever, or so say the coldly clinical folk who write our descriptions of such conditions. One necessary qualification of the coldly clinical is that they must never have suffered from the illness in question, lest their description become considerably more colorful. A less clinical definition of mastitis is a miserably sore breast, the aches and chills that go with fever, and an overall feeling of "Why did this have to happen to me?"

The best treatment for such an ailment is prevention, and most mothers have learned by the time we have been nursing a year or more pretty much what each of us must do and what we must avoid in order not to come down with a breast infection. What seems to bring this problem on varies from individual to individual. Some always have to be very careful about the fit of bras and other clothing. Many have to avoid overexertion or exhaustion. And most have to avoid allowing too long an interval to pass between nursing times.

As your child gets older it continues to be important to remember the things you might do ("nursing indiscretions" Dr. E. Robbins Kimball has named them) that could bring you down with mastitis. For instance, it is tempting to wear that pretty bikini you wore before you were pregnant now that you are all firm and back in shape. Yet you must treat that bikini top the way you would any new bra—with suspicion. If it does not fit you just right, you may not be able to wear it yet.

Avoiding exhaustion is a challenge as long as we are mothers of small children. For some of us there is no more difficult time to keep from overdoing than during our children's second or third year. Frequently our expectations for ourselves increase now that the baby is "older," and people around us begin to expect more, too. Actually you are likely to accomplish more beyond the business of caring for your child in her first year than in her second. Children between one and two, or even between one and three sometimes require more physical exertion on the mother's part than at any other time in their lives. Many of them, besides being busy and needing lots of attention, nurse frequently so that milk production remains at a high level. A mother who undertakes too much—more for some, less for others, depending upon each individual mother's limits—beyond nursing and caring for her child may find herself in bed with a throbbing breast and fever. Coming down with mastitis is not the end of the world, of course, but it is really uncomfortable and should serve as a warning to slow down and not ask so much of yourself right now.

As children grow older, their nursing patterns tend to become less regular, and longer stretches between nursings begin to develop. Sleeping through the night may produce a period of several hours without nursing. Whenever such an interval develops, you need to be aware of your body's reaction. Do your breasts become overfull? Do you begin to feel aches or any sign of breast tenderness?

If so, gently encourage your child to nurse immediately and often to keep the sore breast drained until you feel normal again. Cutting back on the amount of solids that you offer your child for a day or two can help, too. Then avoid the long time between certain nursings for a while by offering to nurse your child maybe a time or two during the night, or during the day—whichever is causing you problems.

Most mothers of children past about the middle of their second year adapt easily to uneven nursing patterns such as nursing only during the day, or only during the evening and night. A few do not. In situations like this we need to realize that a nursing relationship meets needs shown by two people. It is quite right for you to let him drop nursings, and yet also right that you should ask your child for help when you need his nursing to help you avoid an illness.

For almost all mothers well-fitting clothes, adequate rest, and nursing patterns that are not too wildly irregular are all it takes to avoid mastitis. On rare occasion there is a mother, however, who is so subject to breast infection that her body cannot tolerate the normal reduction in nursing frequency that occurs in natural weaning.

If you are in the weaning process and find yourself ill every time your child drops a nursing, first of all you should upgrade your own health and diet and do what you can to get yourself in the best condition possible. Eat better—especially fresh fruits, juices, and vegetables. Suspend some project you have going right now so that you can have time for extra rest and enjoyable exercise. Taking extra care of yourself is a good investment, especially at such a time. Almost always, doing these things will be enough to help you through the weaning period. Only if you continue to have repeated breast infections would it become necessary to take the measures described in the next paragraph.

When you suspect a sore breast is beginning again, encourage your child to nurse frequently until all soreness is gone. Call your doctor if you need to. If he feels you need an antibiotic, take it and continue nursing often. Once you are well, think about the nursing pattern you had before you became ill. Prior to the time your child dropped a feeding (or more than one sometimes) and your breast became sore, how often was she nursing? From that you can figure out the maximum interval between nursings that your body can tolerate. When your child nurses, check the clock, add your maximum time interval to the present time, and make a note—mental or written—of the time you have just calculated. If your child has not asked to nurse by this time, then ask her to nurse. Be sure to do this every time you nurse. Of course you can nurse more frequently, but not less.

You should be able to avoid breast infection by taking life easy and not going too long between nursings. As the weeks go on you will be able gradually to let your child increase the maximum time interval that you can allow without nursing so that she will have the opportunity to move toward weaning in her own time, but still in a way that your body can tolerate.

Not nearly so rare as the mother whose system cannot handle the pace of natural weaning is the mother who takes off on an outing, maybe leaving her child at home, or sometimes even with him along. In the excitement one or both may forget that they usually nurse one or more times, and much to mother's surprise, she has a sore breast the next day. It is wise not to forget that you are a nursing mother on such occasions. Be sure to take time out to nurse or to express milk once or twice while you are out. You will be better off the next day if you do.

BITING

Rarely does a mother make it through an entire nursing career without being bitten at least once. Yet you can be sure that very few children bite very much, or no mother would be willing to nurse, much less enjoy it as most do. The vast majority of children see quickly that they cannot bite if they want to continue nursing.

The most likely time for a child to bite is during the first year, usually in connection with teething at one time or another. Such an incident can occur later, however, and sometimes even with a toddler teething is still involved. Your child is experimenting with using your nipple—inappropriately—to comfort painful gums. You can help by tempering your response to being bitten as much as humanly possible at the time lest you frighten your child away from nursing. Terminate the nursing for a few moments when you are bitten, and talk to your child. Tell him it hurts. Tell him he must nurse gently. Be sure to offer him things he can bite that will comfort his gums. Air drying your nipples the way you may have done when your baby was tiny will probably help if they become tender as the result of a bite.

When you do talk to your child about biting you will need to measure the severity with which you speak according to how sensitive your child is to verbal rebuke and of course according to what you can manage under the circumstances. Not infrequently children will refuse to nurse after having been scolded for biting more harshly than they could cope with (which for some children does not have to be very harsh at all). Some mothers, considering this possibility, especially with children under two or so, make an effort to curb biting without fussing at the child, but with only calm removal from the breast for awhile.

A few children, even if you have taught them not to bite at some previous time, may later experiment playfully with various "stunts," including nipping at your nipple. She may pull your nipple out as far as she can, bite at it, blow it to tickle you, and on and on through all the tricks little ones invent for entertainment. When your child comes up with any game that hurts you, no matter how funny she may think it is, stop the nursing right then. Tell her why you are stopping, and resume nursing when you are satisfied that she has agreed to your terms.

Allow me to reassure you again, your child in either of these instances is almost certain to learn very quickly to nurse without hurting you, though once in a while it is necessary to work for weeks with a child before she gets the message. Perhaps the reason that the vast majority of children learn not to bite so quickly is that we invariably react immediately and firmly to biting at the breast. There is probably no instance in which we apply behavior modification so immediately, decisively, and consistently. Besides, our children love us and respond to the urgency and sincerity with which we insist that they must not bite. Many a child who is old enough to talk will respond when you tell him he has hurt you with a sincere "Sorry Mommy," and a kiss.

A few little people seem to grow bored after nursing a while and then bite. Occasionally a child bites because he is actually hungry. Such biting can be prevented by terminating the nursing when your child first shows signs of restlessness indicating that he would really prefer something else. You can make a point of shortening some nursing sessions a bit and follow these with interesting distractions or food.

Now and then biting can be a clue that your child wants to wean. "You don't have to nurse," one mother told her child who was nipping and playing at the breast. "Are you sure you don't mind, Mommy?" the little girl responded. Apparently this child thought for some reason that she was supposed to nurse at bedtime, even though she was no longer interested. It was certainly time to let the child know, as this mother did, that it is fine for her to wean if she wants to.

Your child may bite for the consistent and predictable reaction he gets from you. Not often, but once in a while the quickest way to stop the biting is to control your reactions— admittedly a difficult plan to carry out. Your child may become bored with the game and go on to something else that is fun for both of you.

It may be that your child is biting because he is upset with you and wants to hurt you. If biting begins at the same time as some change that may be upsetting to your child, you may want to consider the possibility that your child is signaling you for help, in an immature and inefficient way certainly, but signaling nonetheless. One mother whose two-and-a-half-year-old child persisted in biting, initiated the following interchange with her child:

Mom: Why are you biting?
Tot: Don't know.
Mom: Do you want to hurt me?
Tot: Yes.
Mom: Why?
Tot: Don't know.

Mom: Is it because you're angry with me?
Tot: Yes.
Mom: Why are you angry?
Tot: Because hm-hm-hm-hm (Translated that means, I
          don't want to talk about it).
Mom: No, we're going to talk about it. Are you angry
          because the baby's here?
Tot: Yes. (Look of relief)
Mom: I understand how you feel, It's okay.

It is tempting to say that after this conversation all biting disappeared like magic. It did not. From that time on, though, both mother and child understood what was happening and were able to work on helping the child feel better. The biting did diminish, and soon ceased altogether.

If your child is not verbal enough or refuses to enter into this sort of conversation, some sleuthing on your part may help you determine if the biting results from unhappy or angry feelings your child is not handling well. It may help to volunteer to your child that it is okay to be mad at you for having a new baby or for holding him down while he had stitches—or whatever you think might be troubling him. (You aren't admitting that you were wrong in these situations—just letting him know that his feelings about these things are fine and that you accept them and will help him deal with them.) Once in a while that will be all he needs.

Some biting can even be a simple attention-getter, and a very effective one. It is a way that your child can protest against being ignored while she is nursing. Many children at the breast, like many lovers, want to see your eyes. They may especially resent your talking to other people while nursing, but watching television or reading annoy some children. It may eliminate any biting problem you have just to give your attention voluntarily to your child when she nurses. That will also make it possible to see when your child may be about to clamp down so you can slip a finger into her mouth to prevent the bite.

There are also occasions on which biting occurs by acci-dent—for instance when a child is nursing in an awkward position and falls or from a sudden stop when nursing in a moving car. I remember vividly the time when one of mine was nursing while standing on a narrow little bench. She fell, biting my nipple painfully and tipping the bench over onto my toenail, which later developed an ugly black bruise. I found the whole affair quite painful at the time and learned in the future to be more cautious about where and how I let my children nurse. It was almost worth it, though, to be able to watch people's faces when they asked what had happened to my toe. "It is a nursing injury," I told them blankly.

Some children who fall asleep nursing will accidentally bite in their sleep. Not all children do this, and not usually during the first nine months or thereabouts, so there is no reason to worry about this happening unless or until it does. Mothers who are bitten once this way, however, quickly learn not to fall asleep any more while their little ones are nursing, even though sleeping while nursing is such a precious luxury to relinquish. Still, it is not pleasant to be bitten, and it is possible to prevent such accidental biting if need be by staying awake until your little one is sound asleep and then getting your thumb or finger firmly between her teeth and deftly removing your nipple.

Though biting does happen occasionally over the nursing years, we are invariably quick to develop the skills and tactics necessary to keep it from becoming more than an occasional problem.

IF YOU BECOME PREGNANT AGAIN

It is not at all infrequent for a mother to become pregnant before the little child is ready to give up nursing. Becoming pregnant in the first year of nursing is not unheard of (though nursing and/or family-planning techniques can make such early conception quite unlikely) and is quite common in the second and third years. If you do become pregnant while still nursing, you will be faced with the decision of whether or not to wean because of your pregnancy, whether it be for your sake, for the sake of your child, or for the sake of the tiny person inside you, though continued nursing would be in no way harmful to any of you.

It seems to me that the natural thing to do (using "natural" in the strictly biological sense of the word) when you become pregnant is to wean. At this time your body tends to focus itself on the needs of the new baby, and, no matter what you may think about it intellectually, your body's resources and energy are directed toward that baby. The plan of nature seems to be that by the time a mother becomes pregnant again the older child should be mature enough to have his needs met by more people than just his mother and by foods other than her milk. Most of the time when breastfeeding and mothering proceed naturally, this maturity is there. Then the mother will urge her child gently to wean, and because he is ready, weaning will be very easy.

In their study of 503 La Leche League members who became pregnant while still nursing, Niles Newton and Marilyn Theotokatos report that 69% weaned at some time during pregnancy. "How many of these would have weaned if they were not pregnant is not known since no non-pregnant control groups are available. Since the child was getting older, it is likely that even without another pregnancy, there would be a high proportion of weaners."

Children mature at different rates, though. And any number of variables can affect how soon a mother becomes pregnant again. Many mothers who become pregnant when they have a child still nursing, knowing that nature can be cruel to the older child sometimes, decide to continue the nursing

My mommy's nummies are broken.

relationship, or at least to give it a try.

For many mothers this seems the obvious and, no matter what terms I may use, the natural choice. They respond to the immaturity of the child in their arms. They feel strongly that ending the nursing relationship would deny the child advantages that they want for their children.

"I had the problem of deciding whether or not to wean," one mother says. "I had known one or two mothers who had nursed siblings, and I thought that was one thing I'd never do. But I did not anticipate an unplanned pregnancy or babies spaced so closely, either. I ended up deciding that if my son did not wean himself I would keep on nursing him quite willingly. I was very concerned about his being pushed out of the baby position so young. This seemed such a good way of reassuring him of my love."

For many mothers nursing through pregnancy is one of the easiest courses to take. "When I was pregnant, " a mother writes, "and needed to rest, nursing was the only way I could get the baby to lie down with me." Because of the changes that weaning would necessitate in the way these mothers care for their children, it appears to be a much larger hurdle than overcoming any difficulties that might arise because of being pregnant and nursing.

There can be special joys, of course, as well as challenges, in nursing through pregnancy, for example when your child is at the breast enjoying both you and the movements of her new sibling. Sometimes the only negative factor in nursing while pregnant is the surprise or disapproval of people, including medical helpers, who are under the impression that no one ever does such a thing. Some people even suggest that the milk of a pregnant mother will somehow "poison" the child—of course it will not.

For other mothers, nursing through pregnancy is not an easy, spontaneous behavior. According to Newton and Theotokatos, 74% of the mothers in their study experienced nipple discomfort or pain. This is part of the body's adjustment to pregnancy, a condition which does not respond to standard sore nipple treatments. This discomfort may be temporary— only a few days or weeks at some time during pregnancy—or it may last from the third or fourth week after conception until the new baby is born. A smaller number of mothers (30% frequently, 20% rarely or infrequently) also feel very restless when nursing during pregnancy—described by some as an "antsy feeling." This is probably a part of the natural weaning urge in a pregnant mother—a drive to wean by walking away from the nursling as we have all seen some pets do when weaning their little ones. In late pregnancy the child's wriggling and putting pressure on the abdomen is uncomfortable for some mothers. Nursing also causes uterine contractions which bother some mothers, but not others.

If you find yourself pregnant and not happy with nursing, by all means tell your child about your discomfort if he is old enough to understand, and not in a martyred way intended to make her feel guilty for needing to nurse. After all, your child does not want to hurt you and may be quite concerned, as was one three-year-old who told his mother, "I'm sorry if I hurt you when I nurse, Mommy; but my teeth don't make holes." This child, as yours may, needed the reassurance his mother gave him that he was not responsible for her discomfort. At the same time you do want to ask your child for help and cooperation.

You can often work toward an arrangement that is as agreeable as possible for both of you. Remember to give your child plenty of attention besides nursing and also easy access to food and good things to drink. The adjustment the two of you make may lead to total weaning. Or your adjustments may result in very little change at all if your child still shows you a great need for nursing.

Many mothers tell me that the breathing and relaxation techniques they learned in childbirth classes made it easier to cope with any discomfort they felt while nursing. Others distract themselves from their restless, uneasy feelings by reading, watching television, eating or drinking something, or just deliberately thinking of other things while the little child nurses.

Though there is no sure treatment for nipple tenderness during pregnancy, it may help if you are still producing more than a few drops of milk to get the milk flowing a bit by hand-expression before beginning to nurse. Sometimes even if your milk production is minimal it can make nursing less uncomfortable to pull each nipple out gently before nursing to get it erect and reduce the friction when your child begins sucking. For many pregnant mothers, though, only the next change in your body, be that the passing of another week, or the birth of the new baby, will serve as the "cure" for the tender nipples that some pregnancies bring.

Nausea during pregnancy dims some mothers' enjoyment of nursing. It is difficult indeed to manage a bouncing little person when you are feeling that your stomach will turn at the slightest movement. Nursing is not really the problem here, of course; needing to hold your child is the difficulty, and that comes up whether you are nursing or not. Improved diet, extra vitamins, especially vitamin B^6, rest and small, frequent snacks can all help overcome the possible nausea of pregnancy.

Nursing can be something of a lifesaver if you do feel nauseated, for you can lie down beside your child. Caring for him that way is usually much less bothersome to your stomach than not nursing and, therefore, having to carry him, fix food for him, and so on. Even through such difficulties as nausea or tender nipples, many mothers find adequate motivation to persist in nursing in the obvious needs and uninhibited gratitude children show for having their mothers available to them in such a loving way.

If you do find yourself pregnant while seeing a need to continue nursing your child, avoid making any fixed plans about how your nursing relationship will proceed over the next several months. As I have already pointed out, your feelings and tolerances are unpredictable during pregnancy. Children's reactions to pregnancy and the new baby vary a great deal, too. While some do not indicate that they notice any changes because of mother's pregnancy, others tend to wean very early in pregnancy, presumably because of a change in the taste of the milk or a decreased supply. Others react to whatever changes occur in the milk in later pregnancy, sometimes by weaning. Others, though, like one little guy I know, a child who loved to nurse, complain about the "yuck-o milk" but keep on nursing. Sometimes, too, your abdomen in late pregnancy can become so large that your child may find getting to your nipple just too awkward.

As if to add one more bit of confusion to life, there is no way of knowing whether a child who weans during pregnancy will stay weaned once the baby comes and you again have a good supply of milk—and milk that tastes good at that.

One thing I rather hate to bring up, because I feel we do our best when we are motivated by positive rather than negative views of the future, is the fact that a pregnancy is not always uneventful. Mothers have shared their disappointment with me over having weaned a child because of pregnancy when that pregnancy later ended in miscarriage. On the other hand, mothers who have lost their babies at various stages of development have told me what a comfort their nursing child was to them while they were overcoming their disappointment and grief. When the new baby has been born prematurely or is too ill to nurse, the older child's nursing has been a great help in establishing and maintaining a good supply of milk—a boon for the little one who needs that milk so desperately. You will, of course, want to hand-express or pump as much as possible of the colostrum and first milk for the little one before your child nurses. The toddler, then, will take some of the milk, but that is certainly reasonable salary for making the milk let down and flow the way no pump would be able to do.

Some people, understandably enough, wonder whether the uterine contractions stimulated by nursing could actually be the cause of a mother's going into labor too soon. Yet we have years of experience with mothers who have been nursing through pregnancy, even those with a past history of miscarriage and premature delivery and there is no readily apparent increase in either problem.

There is also concern occasionally expressed that the hormones of pregnancy might be harmful to the nursing child. So far as I know, no research has been done into this question to see what hormones, if any, are present in the milk and in what quantities. There seems little reason to worry, though, about natural hormones present at natural levels, especially since we are talking about hormones that tend to reduce the amount of milk the child receives anyway. Besides, the developing fetus is exposed to the very same hormones. I doubt there is any more reason to worry about natural progesterone in the milk during pregnancy than there is to worry about the natural estrogen that is in the milk once the menses have resumed.

NURSING TWO

If your child does continue to nurse all the way through your pregnancy you may be entering into the unique experience of nursing two.

It is an experience that most mothers who have tried it find satisfying; only six percent of the mothers who had tandem nursed reported to Newton and Theotokatos that they would not nurse two again should the occasion arise.

I had to laugh when one mother wrote me, "I guess we're going to try tandem nursing since my son nursed while I was in the early stages of labor." You cannot be sure, even at this point, though, because different children react differently to the return of your milk supply. Some children, just as mom gets adjusted to the idea of having two nurslings, dislike the gushing milk that appears shortly after the birth of the new baby. When that happens, even if mother wants the child to nurse, he will not. Other kids are overjoyed at all the good milk, while still others do not show that they notice any change—though of course they do.

What a kindness and comfort it can be to some children after the birth of that precious new baby—precious, but maybe a bit threatening to them—for their mothers to take them into their arms for that old familiar kind of loving! Your child may be especially grateful if you have been away in the hospital for a while. "We were a little anxious," one mother wrote, "to see what our son's reaction to the new baby's nursing at bedtime, his special time, would be. Dad, mom, and baby (nursing) crawled into bed. Our son stood beside the bed, shifting his weight from one foot to the other. I said, 'Well, come on. Here's your place.' He heaved the biggest sigh, his face lit up, and in he scampered and began to nurse, too. That remains one of my most treasured moments."

Continuing to nurse your child is one way to show him that you still love the baby in him, too. And being a baby when he needs to will help him grow into his big brother role with less conflict. He does not have to be big all the time until he is ready, and he does not have to give you up entirely to the new baby.

We can (and most of us do) help our children make the transition from being the baby of the family to being an older sibling without tandem nursing. Dr. Herbert Ratner's philosophy of babying the baby in the growing child is the critical concept; nursing is one good tool you can use if it is available to you and if you want to.

When a mother approaches nursing two with such lofty motivation, it can be quite a shock if she finds herself unexpectedly experiencing (as so many of us do in this circumstance) waves of resentment at the nursing demands of this suddenly BIG child. Actually, mothers often face the same kinds of feelings towards other demands of their children when there is a new baby, even if their children are not nursing. When nursing is involved, though, negative feelings tend to focus there.

Such feelings in us are actually a part of rearranging and redefining our mothering now that a new baby is part of our lives. During pregnancy we harbor fears that caring for the new baby will "cheat" the young child we already love so much. We also fear that we can never love the coming baby as much as the child in our arms.

Once the baby comes, however, we find that nature has loaded the dice very heavily in the tiny one's favor, especially if we are able to have a really good beginning with our newborns in the first hours and days. In just a few hours most of us feel transformed from a guardian angel, determined never to allow an intruder to change our current parent-child relationship, into a primitive mother, keyed to defending the newborn's prerogatives at all costs.

Not all mothers experience such a dramatic shift in feelings, but many do and suffer needless alarm and guilt. Once our feelings have swung like a tire-on-a-rope from one side of the yard to the other, they will moderate to a more functional middle place. Our love for each child will develop—different, rich, exciting. We give our love as one candle gives its flame to another. Though we give all our love to one child, as if by magic we still have our love left to give to the next, and to the next (Zilberg).

If you do find yourself for the baby's sake resenting your child's nursing, be reassured that what you are feeling is shared by mothers here and there all over the world right now. Feeling this way does not mean that you will never enjoy nursing your child again.

Considering the fact that your child may also be going through a mixed-up time right now, I would suggest that for some children this may not be a good time to talk much to them about your negative feelings. You and your child will benefit from a few weeks of nursing with as little conflict as possible while you adjust to your new family setup.

You may feel especially anxious about whether your new baby will get enough milk. There may be a strong urge to restrict your toddler's nursing to certain times of day or to nursing only after the baby has finished. If such restrictions work out easily for your children, it is fine to employ them with caution. Limiting the toddler's nursing is occasionally necessary if he consistently wants to nurse right before the baby awakens. After all, the baby has to have the milk and the toddler does not. But such situations are not common. Most mothers nursing two find that they produce plenty of milk to nurse the baby and the toddler, each whenever he likes. It is ever so much easier to forget about the milk and pay attention to mothering these little people. After all, you could completely feed twins on demand.

One of the attractive reasons for nursing siblings is that this is one tool you can employ toward reduced sibling rivalry. If nursing becomes one more of the many pleasures in life over which your children have to contend with each other, taking turns and that sort of thing, then it may become part of their struggle with each other for their places in your affection. "Oh, wow, it'll be all gone then," griped one two-year-old asked to wait until the baby was through. It is in the families who have felt free to allow both baby and toddler to nurse on demand that the low level of conflict between the children has been most dramatic.

From the viewpoint of nutrition, too, it seems best not to employ an unchanged pattern for nursing, always nursing one first and the other afterwards. For your milk is different at different times in a feeding. If your young toddler nurses frequently and always last, then the baby may not get his share of the rich hind-milk. The baby needs both the fluid and the water-soluble nutrients early in each feeding and also the fats and fat-soluble nutrients nearer the end. If you nurse them with a less rigid pattern, the baby will get the proper balance of nutrients over the course of the day. The baby, being the more frequent nurser, should have "first grabs" more often than not, but he needs to have some opportunities at "finishing up" too. If you can relax and not try to structure your children's nursing patterns, they will work out their own and without the problems we may cause when we interfere.

It is wise, though, to be a bit conscious for your own sake of the frequency of your toddler's nursing and not to let him vary the frequency so widely from day to day that your breasts become overfull some days, particularly if you are prone to breast infections anyway. The great fluctuation in frequency of nursing that is common in nursing children is usually not much of a problem when your milk supply is waning. But when you are fully nursing a baby, you may need to encourage your nursing child not to get distracted and let your breasts get too full. You may not, of course, be affected if your child nurses several times one day, and not at all the next. But if you are, do not hesitate to encourage him to nurse when he has forgotten to ask for too long a time.

Baby carriers—the soft kind that hold the baby against your body—are great helpers when caring for one little one. When you have two needing your time and attention, I would regard a carrier as almost indispensable. You can cuddle the little one in the carrier while still seeing to your bigger, but still little one. Your child may especially appreciate it if you can learn to carry your baby on your back part of the time, rather than in front, so that you are not having to work over and around the baby when you tend to your child. Having plenty of attention from you will help keep your toddler's need for attention through nursing at the minimum level for him.

If difficulties develop with either nursling—any of the difficulties you might encounter in nursing either one of them alone, you may be called upon for extra creativity in coping with both children's needs—and with your own. One mistake we often make, though, is thinking of the nursing relationships we have with nursing siblings as one relationship, when in fact it is two separate nursing relationships. Yes, you are the same mother, and the little people do interact. But the nursing relationships are individual with each child.

The baby is not likely to have colic because his big sister is still nursing, nor will big sister go on much of a nursing binge exclusively because of the baby's nursing; she is probably expressing needs for other attention and perhaps food as well as anxiety over the amount of mother's time and energy that the new baby needs. Because tandem nursing is unfamiliar to us, even more so than toddler nursing, it is quite easy to say that such-and-such is happening because both are nursing. The truth is, however, that baby may have colic for whatever reasons there may be that babies have colic, and big sister may want to nurse all the time for the kinds of reasons that other people her age sometimes want to nurse all the time. We still have to look at each child as an individual and do the best we can to help each one when we need to.

The arrival of a new baby, like any one of many events in

the life of your child, can cause her to need extra time at your breast. Though it may be quite a challenge for you for a while, especially with the new baby to care for, too, tending to her as completely as you can will be your easiest course in the long run. Of course extra loving from daddy will be a big help in meeting the needs of your children, especially the toddler. His loving can be administered directly to the children and also indirectly through his love and support for you at a demanding time like this.

Nursing two in the presence of other people is not often necessary, for the older child is usually busy and distractable when you are away from home. There are situations that arise, though, when neither can wait and there is no privacy to be found, situations when you are best sustained by self-confidence and a sense of humor. A mother of a three-month-old baby and a two-and-a-half-year-old child wrote of such an incident:

> On the plane they both wanted to nurse at the same time, but the two-and-a-half-year-old had to nurse standing up— no other way would do—much to the astonishment of the two little old ladies beside us! It was all we could do to keep from laughing aloud, and my husband pretended he didn't know us. But both children were happy!

Many a mother who has worried about how she would feel should she need to nurse both her little ones away from home has been relieved to be able to find a place to nurse alone, or has been gratified that her little ones cooperated beautifully and were surprisingly discreet. Nursing siblings "in public" is a problem usually more in anticipation than in reality.

Sometimes mothers worry about cross-infection from nursing two children—like letting them use the same toothbrush. Actually our children live so close together in the same environment that preventing cross-infection is nearly impossible. In addition, the anti-bacterial properties of the milk itself probably work to prevent cross-infection.

The only common ailment for which it might be advisable to confine each child to one breast is if one of them contracts thrush. Your pediatrician can help you find the most effective treatment for this fungus infection in your baby. It may be necessary to treat your breasts also in order to prevent or relieve the soreness the infection can cause and to bring it under control. Your physician may also recommend a vaginal test for you to see whether the organism is causing vaginitis as well as thrush. Your doctor can help you decide whether both children need treatment, or if you can watch the one who is not affected and start treatment only if symptoms appear.

In general, though, the only way to prevent cross-infection is to keep people from living together in anything so "unsanitary" as a family, doing such things as eating and breathing together. I cannot believe that whether they both nurse or not is going to cause much, if any, increase in their rate of infection.

How either of these little guys is ever going to wean if he sees the other one nursing is a very common and understandable worry. We have been schooled to think of nursing as a bad habit which will go on forever if we do not somehow eliminate the opportunities for nursing and get the child to forget about it. But nursing is not a sneaky way little people have of dominating adults. Rather it is the manifestation of infantile needs in the growing child. When children wean spontaneously it is not because they forget about it, but because they have outgrown the need.

As I have said before, we must remember even when nursing two that we are nursing individual children. Rivalries between siblings over nursing and nursing only because the other is nursing are uncommon as long as both can come to you freely most of the time, whenever they feel the need to nurse.

When they will wean naturally is determined by their own individual development and will not be changed much if any by seeing the sibling nurse. There are likely to be changes and adjustments in nursing because of pregnancy and getting used to life with the new baby. But once these normal crises are past, each child should settle into the kind of nursing pattern he would have if he were the only one nursing. Usually the older one will get into his pattern of nursing again, and gradually lose interest over the months or years until he just quits asking. Meanwhile the baby continues in his own individual pattern.

It is not uncommon for mothers to find themselves nursing two toddlers at once (not as difficult as it sounds, because the older one is usually becoming so much less demanding all the time). It is not unheard of for both children to wean about the same time or for the younger one to wean first, but neither of these instances is the usual.

In a few families in which the older child has needed some nursing for several years, a second younger sibling has arrived while the older two were still nursing. No doubt someone has loved and cared for four who were not completely weaned. I shudder at pointing out these unusual situations lest I contribute to some sort of inter-mother rivalry over who can have the most children nursing at once. Such a contest would be nonsense, and, besides, children are not likely to cooperate by nursing once they have outgrown the need anyway. What I do want to communicate here is a help for mothers in seeing that it is possible to look at the needs of each child as an individual as well as a member of a family. It can be a kindness to a child to allow him to outgrow baby things at his own pace, even when little brothers and sisters join the family. Our children do not get bigger all of a sudden when a new baby arrives; they just look bigger to us!

CHAPTER 10

For Fathers —You Are Parents, Too

As a father you are interested in growing the best children you can—children who are healthy and independent. Also you want children who love you and are glad they have you for their father. What a blessing it is to you and to your children to know that you can use the very approaches that make your children love you—gentleness and tenderness—to help them grow strong. From the solid base of your love your children can face any challenge they need to.

It is hard sometimes when your children are very young to see their love for you developing. Many children, of course, are quite responsive and show affection for dad from the beginning; how pleasant such tiny babies are. But many others focus their attention almost exclusively on mother for a painfully long time. You can feel rejected and left out if you let yourself, especially with your first child.

You should not let those unhappy feelings grow larger, though, for they are in response to a problem (if you want to call it a problem) that is growing smaller all the time. Think about how immature your child is—how much she has to learn. She has to figure out how to love and trust one person before she can love and trust many people. If you are the person, next to her mother, who is around her the most in a warm way, but not pushy, you will probably be the very next person she opens up to, just as soon as she can.

If you want to hasten the time when your child will trust you and enjoy playing with you, you might try making yourself available in rather unorthodox manners. One way psychiatrist-father Hugh Riordan, a frequent speaker before parents' groups, suggests that fathers make contact with shy children is to lie quietly on the floor. Once they can move about he says that children, like puppies, usually cannot resist climbing all over you as long as you stay quiet enough not to make them shy away. Of course as your child grows older such play can evolve into as much roughhouse as you and your child want. It may need to start very calmly, though.

Another way to get your child's attention is to sit on the floor and play with his toys—not the ones he is playing with of course. When you do this he may continue to play alongside you, or join you, or snatch the toys away from you; any of these games can be fun for both of you. Some fathers win over their babies even earlier by coming close when the child is nursing, tempting her to reach out to you. When she does offer you a tiny hand or foot, you can kiss it or give it a little tickle, thereby beginning the loving games you will be playing more and more over the months and years ahead.

The most fundamental and permanently effective way to hasten the time when your child will be the fun companion you may have dreamed of is perhaps the opposite of what you might think at first. Do what you can to encourage and help your wife function as a mother to your child. Encourage her to nurse him and help her to baby the baby in him for as long as there is any baby left in him. Your wife, like so many, will rejoice in your support. "I remember the pride my husband showed when I nursed," one mother wrote; and the whole family is no doubt stronger because of that father's warmth and support.

You can help make it easy for your wife to provide the mothering your child needs, or you can make it nearly impossible. With your help your child can make the best beginning possible toward being a charming and resourceful addition to your life.

You and your wife need to discuss your parenting goals, not just once, but periodically. You will not always agree on every little point, but life will be much easier if you are working essentially toward the same goals and supporting each other. When you do not see eye to eye, at least you can each be aware of the other's viewpoint so as not to undermine each other. Your discussions need not even be aimed at reaching 100% agreement on everything to do with your children (or anything else for that matter). Among the benefits children gain from a home with two parents is an ability to live with differing viewpoints and inconsistencies which are an unavoidable part of human life. Your discussions will help you keep your focus on general goals so that you can know how to help each other when you encounter difficulties.

Just as your wife will help you, so you need to help her keep on the track you have chosen, particularly when you are not following the same general procedures as the people around you. You can be a crucial factor in helping your child grow up well by supporting your wife in questions concerning toilet training and bedtimes (or lack thereof), and especially when nursing is involved. You can be her best source of support, or encouragement, and of the mature judgment sometimes necessary to make it as easy as possible for her to nurse your child as long as he needs it.

Mothers say that the most difficult problems they face in nursing past infancy result from criticism from other people—family, friends, medical helpers. Sometimes this pressure, almost always from people who are as well-intentioned as they are misinformed, can be great enough to break a mother's resolve to have the best possible beginning with your child. You can protect your wife, and thereby protect your child's birthright, by reminding her of your support for what she is doing. You can also put a stop to the conversations that bother her, occasionally, by explaining what she is doing and why.

Usually, though, there is no need to try to bring other people around to your way of childrearing; it is more efficient most of the time to change the subject of conversation firmly and unrelentingly. Some parents who find that certain associates persist in the rudeness of criticizing their parenting decisions simply find new friends who are either more compatible in their opinions or at least have better manners.

Your wife will probably need your help most in dealing with any pressure that may come from members of your family. In her own growing up she has probably found ways to deal with her relatives. But she may be a bit unsure of how to communicate with your family and, besides, she does not want to embarrass or offend you. She will certainly benefit from any help you give her in establishing herself as a good and competent mother in the eyes of your family.

There are times, too, when you may need to exercise mature judgment in helping your wife and child make the best of their relationship. Most of us tend to get very involved in traditions (like huge holiday dinners) or family business (like putting up friends and relatives who come through town) or progress (like moving across country). All these involvements can be fun and satisfying when we are able to devote our energy to them without feeling torn in two because of other needs pulling at us too.

There is also the well-published notion that your marriage cannot flourish unless you have a periodic weekend, if not a whole week, away from your little one. The truth is that since you and your wife loved each other enough to produce your child, you are probably quite capable of figuring out plenty of ways to enjoy each other without leaving a child who is too immature yet to be without your love and protection. Chances are you can deal even with social and financial obligations without depriving your young child, and indeed yourself and your wife, of the reliable family intimacy you all need at this time in your child's life.

You may even need to apply a cool, creative mind to such activities as going out in the evening without your child. There may be times you need to take him along, times when you need to go out later, after he is asleep, or times when you find ways to entertain yourselves at home. You should not stop having fun together by any means; you just need to be flexible and inventive when the old ways for now are not in the best interests of your family.

It will make life easier, too, if you spend some time thinking about the things you and your wife have "always done" or the things you have "always wanted to do." When there is a baby or young child around, sometimes it will serve your growing family to put some traditions and dreams off for a year or two. There is likely to be little lost in so doing that you cannot regain later. It is worthwhile to invest heavily in your family, for you want these people to be your family for the rest of your life.

Another way you can provide the best for your child is to help his mother through the times when mothering him well is difficult for her. No doubt she will do the same for you when you become weary and exasperated with some of your

Daddy got hair on his num-nums.

tasks as a father. Many a mother, myself included, has become tired and annoyed with the child's insistence upon nursing at times. How grateful we are for husbands who calm us and gently stick up for our children when we mothers are not at our best. How many evenings I have been set back on track by my husband's mild chiding, "She *needs* to nurse!"

When your wife complains about nursing, as doubtless she will some time, she needs you to slow her down, help her to take some other pressure off herself. (Has she suddenly decided all the closets need cleaning this week? Or started writing a book? Or making holiday plans?) Remind her of what you both want life in your family to be like, and why you want to meet your child's needs as fully as possible. Help her to get her priorities straight again.

There is an impulse when she complains about nursing to write the nursing off as "her thing" and urge her to abandon it and get back to life the way it used to be. If you evaluate the impulse, though, you will see that it is an understandable, immature kind of thought that we all have when something seems difficult. It is an impulse to be put aside as unusable under the circumstances. Now that a child has become part of your lives, there is no returning to things as they were, nor would you want to really.

Nursing is not merely "her thing," but part of your whole family scene. Considering that nursing is something she does for a lot more reasons than her own entertainment, perhaps it should not be surprising how resentful she is likely to be if you respond to her complaints with the suggestion that she wean. Her complaints may be a plea for help from you in caring for your child, or for help in figuring out how to make her life with him easier. One thing is certain: Her complaints are almost always a plea for your reassurance and support for her continued nursing.

Besides, weaning is not an easy solution to the difficulties that can be a part of life with a young child. In fact it is neither easy nor is it a solution. Nursing or not, a young child needs much of her mother's time and attention, and mothers tire of pushing swings and fingerpainting just as easily as they tire of nursing. Weaning a child who does not want to be weaned can also be quite an undertaking. It is sometimes exhausting for both parents and cannot always be accomplished without some emotional damage to the child or even the parents.

It may seem strange at first, but the way to be closest to your wife is to do everything in your power to help her to be close to your child. If you allow yourself to compete with him for her attention, you set up barriers between yourself and her that are hard to break down. You can, instead of seeking attention by coming between your wife and your child, stand beside them and nurture their love for each other. There are great advantages to being the kind of father of whom one woman wrote, "My husband learned about the baby's needs, my needs, giving up some attention from me for her security—but he also learned that his generosity gained him a close relationship with both of us. We are truly devoted to him." As a result of fostering closeness among the members of your family you are likely to be rewarded with increased love and affection from your wife and with an emotionally healthy child—a child who is able to love you as one of the most special people in his world for the rest of his life.

PART III

Nursing
Your
Toddler
—Year by Year

CHAPTER 11

Nursing
in the
Second Year

THE NURSING TODDLER—A BABY ON WHEELS

Somewhere in the development of our culture emerged the strange idea that babyhood ends with the beginning of walking and talking, and that with proper parental management, babyhood can end rather abruptly on the child's first birthday. Instead of standing in proper awe of the accomplishments that babies begin to make around the beginning of their second year, we added demands for more. In addition to making the big changes from crawling to walking and from body language and crying to talking, we also insisted that they be toilet trained, sleep all night by themselves, and leave the bric-a-brac alone.

If we stop to examine a one-year-old child, the absurdity of these demands on them seems obvious. They are what someone has described as "babies on wheels," still infants, but mobile and therefore quite vulnerable. Their little foreheads remain babyishly high and broad; their legs are short and often still bowed; and they continue to have infants' round little bellies. The diapers or pants that stayed on pretty well while they were prone tend to fall victim to gravity now that they are vertical. They look like babies and act like babies. They will be three or four before their bodies and faces have stretched out and straightened into the shapes and propor-

130

tions of childhood. The appearance of these mobile little people still makes us feel we are dealing with babies and, unless we are talked out of it by "experts," we will respond to them in a way appropriate to the care of babies for as long as their babyish appearance and mannerisms continue.

Nursing a child in his second year seems a reasonable way to help meet some of his continuing baby needs. How long he will nurse, how often, etc., is totally unpredictable. Some little ones this age are too busy with exploring to be bothered with much need to nurse. Some are happier to eat the family's food and nurse only to go to sleep or when they are hurt. Some even wean during the second year.

By far the most usual behavior for a child in the second year, however, is to nurse a lot. According to a study done in an area of New Guinea where extended nursing was the norm, nursing continued at frequent enough intervals for mothers to continue producing twenty ounces of milk daily into the third year (Becroft). A child who has nursed less and less frequently near the end of her first year will often surprise her mother by seeming to nurse like a newborn at times during the second year. We all need to be aware of how common and normal frequent nursing is at this time of life. I feel certain mothers would be less distressed by their toddlers' seemingly constant needs to nurse if they were prepared for these needs and knew they are normal and temporary.

As children begin to walk and explore, they meet all kinds of new, unfamiliar situations. They become frightened by new things—to them—that we never dream are frightening. They overextend themselves in their efforts to master new skills, even though we adults may not be aware that they are "working." All that babbling or patting or digging or running around is serious work in the business of growing up.

Some children handle their work with ease, pace themselves well, and cope well with their inevitable frustrations right from the beginning. Most are much more easily distressed and disoriented, especially when facing a new task like walking, and tend to venture too far and get hurt easily.

This busy time of life is wearing on mothers as well as on children. One mother showed her own appreciation for her child's time at her breast saying, "Nursing gives me a break from having to be constantly monitoring his latest activity, which is usually more daring than he realizes." Rapidly learning toddlers usually have urgent and frequent needs for reassurance and encouragement in the feeling that they are progressing well and that it is safe and worthwhile to try again.

The child who needs much nursing is just as likely to grow up emotionally stable and capable as is the child whose needs for help in coping with the world are less intense. Each child grows at his own rate emotionally just as he does physically and intellectually. Nor do we as parents have much to say about what kind of child we will have at this age. We can minimize their anxiety level by meeting their needs as fully as possible from birth on. But how much intense parenting they need, possibly including frequent nursing, in the second year depends for the most part on their inborn timetable for emotional development. As parents we can slow down emotional growth by leaving needs unmet. But there is nothing extra we can do to speed it up.

As difficult as it is to meet the needs of an easily upset toddler, our objective must be to help him grow into a child with the poise and self-confidence which will enable him to cope well with the world of school children and learning he will be meeting at age five or six. Our children do not need this kind of confidence at age one—or even three or four. We have several years to help them grow. There is no hurry, and your investment in your toddler who seems to be "always attached" will pay off when the time for independence does come.

PICKING A CODE WORD

The second year is usually the time to begin thinking about your nursing code word if you are going to use one. Whatever word you pick, you should use it regularly with your child during this year or the next as he begins to talk. That will help you by allowing you to choose what nursing will be called in your family rather than leaving it up to your child's choice as time goes on, and it will help your child by giving a name to something important to him.

NURSING LEAVES ONE HAND FREE

If not in the first year, then certainly in the second, most children find a favorite pastime for their "top" hand as they are nursing. (Until they start doing "acrobatic nursing," they usually lie on the other hand.) They stroke mother's face, force their fingers into her mouth, fiddle with her hair, caress her neck, twiddle or pinch the other nipple, play with mother's belly-button, pummel her with a little fist, and on and on. During your child's first and second year especially you need to be aware of the activities your child develops with that free hand and give some thought to how you feel about them. What he does with that free hand will likely become an integral part of his nursing as time goes on, and getting him to change this activity later can be quite difficult—not always impossible, but difficult. Not frequently children continue to enjoy their individual "free-hand game" whenever they are in mother's lap, even long after they have weaned from the breast.

By far the most common pastime for that free hand is playing with the other nipple. Many mothers find this nipple stimulation very annoying, especially as the child gets older, and some babies pinch painfully. It is not difficult to distract a baby from any game that you dislike if you are aware that whatever she is experimenting with now can become a permanent part of nursing. Having been annoyed by my first nursing toddler's play with my other nipple, and then with her scratching at my navel with little fingernails, with later babies, I was quick to redirect tiny hands (and feet!) from where I did not want them to be for the next few years.

With my child for whom I discovered the need for "redirection" too late, I had to resort to clothing that kept most of my body inaccessible to her little fingers and fingernails. This was not difficult during the day, but it took longer to find a solution for nighttime. At last I came up with a scoop-neck gown with elastic in the neckline that was just firm enough so that she had to hold it with both hands in order to keep it out of the way while she nursed. What a relief that was!

With some children, activity is rarely confined to one hand. They move their whole bodies without losing the nipple. "He was a little monkey," one mother said of her son. "He tried and probably invented twenty positions to nurse in." On occasion you may want to discourage some of the acrobatics too if they should seem dangerous or become uncomfortable for you.

Rather than being negative about his activities while nursing, though, you can be observant and encourage your child toward habits you both enjoy—patting the other breast or mother's cheek are pastimes many mothers like. You should also consider whether or not what your child chooses to do will be acceptable to you when there are other people around, for it is the play while nursing rather than the nursing itself that mothers often find embarrassing around others.

Some mothers point out, of course, that they like the baby to do such things as nurse and play with the other nipple. If that is the case with you, by all means enjoy it! There has got to be some natural reason why so many babies want to do it, and the reason no doubt is that it feels good to both mother and child. The same is true for the regular dental exams many toddlers provide while nursing. Some mothers hate them while others love them. The whole point is, begin to teach your child what you yourself are comfortable having him do with that free hand as soon as he starts exploring with it.

GETTING THROUGH THE PEAK TIME FOR CRITICISM

The second year is the period in which you are most likely to encounter questions and criticism about your little one's continued nursing. He is, as I have said, still very much a baby and still likely to find himself needing to nurse anywhere and everywhere, without regard to how you feel about the people nearby. This is not true for all nurslings this age, but for most of them it is. Few one-year-olds have the verbal or social understanding to respond reliably to explanations and delays. With babies in the second year it is frequently easier and more peaceful, and certainly kinder to the child, just to nurse whenever and wherever he needs it, and deal as pleasantly as you can with any questions or criticism you receive on those occasions when privacy is just not available.

It is too bad that we must cope with something so unnatural as a widespread belief that we should not nurse our babies, and that our one-year-olds are not babies anyway. For little people in their second year offer their parents so much pleasure with their wide-eyed trust and exuberance. If we can rise above any criticism we may meet, we can enjoy our babies as babies far longer than many people think possible or advisable. How satisfying it is for babies—and for parents—not to have to rush through babyhood, no matter who says we should.

CHAPTER 12

Nursing
through the
Terrible Twos

TERRIBLE TWOS—NO LONGER TERRIBLE

A wonderful thing seems to be happening in our world lately. The Terrible Twos are being renamed—"Tantalizing Twos" or "Terrific Twos" some parents now call little people in their third year. And a high percentage of those two-year-olds who have caused their parents to rename their stage of growth are still nursing.

Two-year-olds have earned a reputation for independent thinking and exploration through almost every minute they are awake. Their ambitions far exceed their capabilities, and they have been known to kick and scream out their frustrations in tantrums. Even with the careful watching required to keep them safe, they still get hurt and bring mother fingers and knees that need kisses and ceremonial bandages. They have no patience with adult schedules and the adult pace of life. Their drive to explore is constant, and they protest against being rushed past anything that catches their eyes, be it the neighbor's dog or one of those maddening candy and gum displays at the supermarket check-out line.

All these behaviors in the third year are normal and reflect the exciting growth of their baby minds toward childhood. We do a two-year-old quite a disservice if we become upset by his behavior at this age and try to teach him to behave much differently. He should be inquisitive and eager to try new things—new things of his choice, not ours as we might wish on some of his especially busy days. He should begin to assert himself and make his wishes and opinions known. As he matures he will begin to learn that if he does not get his way right now it does not mean that he will never get his way again. But for now his newly discovered power to make his own decisions is precious, and he will fight anybody, anywhere if he fears he is going to lose that power.

The wise parent learns to work with this new assertiveness, not against it. You are not facing a potential lifelong kind of behavior that must be "nipped in the bud." Rather, you are watching an essential step in the development of a strong and healthy mind. Your child will move on to more reasoned and reasoning behavior over the next few years.

During the fascinating, frustrating, always volatile third year, mothers and children alike find nursing to be a much appreciated leveler. Children use nursing to help calm themselves when mounting tensions—traumas or triumphs, either one—start to become too much for them and make them uncomfortable. Mothers use nursing to calm their children when upset.

Many children this age are weaned and are happy about it. Others nurse only to help themselves fall asleep or wake up. Others use nursing to help themselves get over rough spots at other times during the day. Quite a few children this age still need to nurse rather often. Mothers with two-year-olds still nursing sometimes talk of feeling overwhelmed with how much their children still need them. Others tell how much they enjoy the nursing times. "It's the only time I get to cuddle her or see her sitting still" is a typical comment.

TANTRUMS

Nursing is an especially helpful tool in avoiding a two-year-old's (or any age's) possible tantrums. You or your child can usually recognize that a situation is becoming too tense for the child to handle and initiate nursing. It would be fascinating to know how many tantrums have *not* occurred because of nursing mothers' timely intervention, but that of course is a statistic that will always be shrouded, like the number of cavities prevented by avoiding sweets or the number of colds not caught by people who get the right combination of vitamins, rest, and exercise. If, however, you do find yourself facing a full-fledged tantrum, nursing will probably help you and your child to shorten it and come out of it more peacefully than anything else you can do.

Whenever you find that your child is crying but not too far out of control, you may be able to bring him out of it by making funny faces and jokes, by tickling, or by picking him up to nurse. When your child does get well into a tantrum, something some nursing mothers tell me they have never experienced, he will probably not let you touch him, much less nurse. In that case, sit as near to him as he will let you. Tell him you are there whenever he is ready to nurse. You might see whether he will let you stroke his leg or rub his back; if he will, that is a good start toward calming him.

If not, then find something to do that will keep you from being bored and tempted to walk away from your very frightened and unhappy child. (Yes, I know, the tantrum is probably over something silly—the cat won't stay on the couch, or he can't go to work with daddy—but these things can become terribly huge and overwhelming in a young mind.) Pick up a book. Grab your knitting or that article you were writing for *The Atlantic*—whatever. You can go about your business quietly, as long as you stay put and do not look at him. (Most children in full-blown tantrums are embarrassed along with all their other overwrought feelings and prefer that you not look at them.)

After a while he will probably come sheepishly to you. This is difficult for him to do, and he needs your open arms and ready comfort, not a discussion of the tantrum and the events that led up to it. If he is still nursing, just hold him and let him nurse. Soon a good giggling and tickling session may be in order. If, instead of coming to you for nursing and for loving, he falls asleep where he is lying, you can assume that sleepiness was a contributing cause of the upset. Let him sleep and go about your business, cuddling him and nursing him when he awakens if that is what he seems to want.

Of course tantrums do tend to occur at busy, hectic, often hungry times of the day when it is difficult to stop what you are doing and stay near your unhappy little one. In fact, that is probably how the situation got out of control in the first place. If supper is about to burn on the stove or you have to pick up the older kids at school, you are in one of those situations so common in motherhood in which your family's different needs are pulling you in separate directions.

All you can do is to work through the situation with the best effort you have in you that day (go ahead and pull the pots off the stove before you settle down near your child, or carry your crying child to the car and do the best you can to comfort her in her harness or safety seat). These conflicts of needs are a challenge for all of us from time to time, and everyone seems to survive.

If you find that tantrums are occurring rather consistently at one time of day or in certain circumstances, though, you should look hard at what is going on and apply some parental brilliance to making life a little easier for your child right then. Can that particular bit of business be eliminated or moved to another time or place? What about trying to read a story or nurse beforehand? How long since she has eaten? Perhaps food and/or extra attention will fortify your child enough for her to be able to cope better.

TALKING ABOUT NURSING

One of the joys of nursing a two-year-old is hearing what they have to say on the subject. Some of them will tell you not only when they want to nurse, but exactly where and how—"Not in bed, on couch!" "Don't pull up shirt; open buttons." One little one preferred to open mom's bra herself and would shout "Self! Self!" if mom started·to unhook. At a La Leche League meeting where mothers were nursing their babies, a toddler ran to mother and said brightly, "Oh, many babies num-num; me too!" Occasionally a two-year-old comes to a profound conclusion such as, "Milk inside Mommy!" What charming first steps these little people reveal in their beginning understanding of cultural anthropology and basic physiology.

It is during the third year too that most children become verbal enough to understand a little more of what mother has to say about nursing and to begin to adjust their requests for nursing toward times and places that are the most comfortable for the whole family. This is not to say that there is no

Look, Mommy, that lady has ninny, too!

point in saying anything about nursing to your child before her second birthday or that you will definitely have everything perfectly worked out by the time she turns three. In that vague, general time frame we must use in discussing individuals who develop at such widely different rates, the third year is when we are able to see some results from our attempts at setting limits and helping the child understand them.

It was when her child was about this age that one mother said, "I did insist that reading a newspaper on the floor did not mean I wanted to nurse." Another mother when her child was past two was no longer willing for him to nurse instead of eating supper. She made this change mostly by not sitting down until he had begun to eat. On those occasions on which he still wanted to interrupt his mother's meal, she usually gently insisted upon her right to finish.

We make changes in nursing "rules" the same way we make other changes. We should explain to the two-year-old, for instance, about staying inside the front door rather than running outside into the street. But he will be three or four at least before we will be able to expect him always to observe that rule. The twos are a time of beginnings, not the age at which we get everything settled once and for all.

With your two-year-old you can begin to see results when you explain situations in which nursing makes you uncomfortable—but not all at once, and not 100% reliably. It is best not to try to get her to understand several different changes you want to make all at once or suddenly jump in with restrictions on nursing when you have imposed none before. It is best to be talking about nursing all along, starting in infancy. Then you can be kind of open to opportunities for changing this or that item or discussion from discussion to reality.

The time will come for instance when you can say, "I don't like to nurse at grandma's house. Let's wait until we get into the car," and your child will agree to the plan with a conspiratorial grin, or at least permit you to distract him easily with a toy or a glass of juice. You can suggest to your child nursing at night that she get finished because mommy is sleepy. You can tell your child when he wants to nurse, say, right after supper when you would love to sit down a few minutes with your coffee and needlework, "Daddy will play with you for a little while; then we'll nurse" (or whatever you call it). These suggestions are not likely to be effective at all for quite some time after you begin making them. But someday they will be.

When your child does respond to a request you make about nursing, be sure to praise him and thank him. He is making a positive step in learning to fit his needs in around those of others. It will take him his whole life to learn the art of meeting his own needs without interfering with the needs of others. He is just beginning, and what a praiseworthy event it is.

Occasionally you may find it necessary to impose limits on nursing without waiting for your child to agree with the change. For example, if you should have to be away from your child for a while, then he will not have the opportunity to nurse at certain times of the day no matter what his needs might be. Or you could find that for the sake of other family members you have to be busy sometimes when your child might choose to nurse. In such cases you should do your best to tend to what has to be done and explain to your child as best you can. You will probably be surprised how well such little children often adapt to waiting when you really have to do something else. They seem to understand necessity remarkably well if you are completely honest with them about it. You need to do everything in your power, of course, to see that your child's needs are met—perhaps at other times or even by other people, including father and siblings sometimes—but met fully.

The way you can tell whether you are succeeding in taking care of his needs is to watch him and to give him opportunities to tell you or show you how he is feeling. As long as he continues to grow and learn and is happy most of the time, you can be comfortable with the limits you have set. If he is upset or shows regressive behavior, you need to make special opportunities to baby him or make extra efforts to return to the old routine for a while if at all possible.

Any time you introduce a new "law," either by persuasion or by decree, you need to realize that it may be premature. If you find your child unable to handle new limits you either suggest or impose, do not despair. You need not repeal the law altogether. Just postpone its effective date a few weeks and then try again. You child is growing all the time and after a while will indeed reach the maturity to be able to live comfortably in your family's routine.

FREQUENT NURSING IN A TWO-YEAR-OLD

The third year is usually a period in which children find many other things to do besides nursing, even the ones who seem to nurse like newborns in their second year. Some stop nursing altogether. Often they are just as intense about needing to nurse as they ever were, but the need strikes them less often.

Occasionally a mother asks about a two-year-old who still seems to want to nurse all the time. The first thought about a child this age who still expresses a need for so much nursing is that we have probably just set up a new timetable for growth that does not fit this child.

We must keep in mind, too, that two-year-olds are demanding people. They need a great deal of mother's attention, and nursing is one way to get that attention. Nor is getting your attention an evil plot against you by your child; she needs your attention, and a lot of it. Children this age can also need a lot of extra nursing because of boredom (in their terms, not ours—little children's interests vary as widely as do other people's). Or some children can need to nurse a lot because of overstimulation or having to face up to situations that are still too much for them.

If you have a two-year-old who needs to nurse more frequently than most (more than the very common pattern at
this age: waking, bedtime, once or twice during the night,
naptime, and any time you sit or lie down), you might take a
good look at what is going on at your house. What kind of
attention is your child getting from you? Having mother there
with lots of closeness and cuddling is still nice—just the way
it was in more babyish times, but your budding genius needs
more now. He announces his new ambitions clearly: "Me do
it!" His hungry little mind will devour the activities and
materials available to him at a good preschool—except that
few little ones this age can be comfortable enough away from
mother to make use of even the most fantastic facilities and
program in the world.

So for a while the family needs to provide the "preschool." Maybe you will utilize all the clever ways mothers
have always entertained two-year-olds, mostly by doing only
what has to be done around the house, but doing these things
slowly and teaching the little one how to help. Some children
need lots of paints and crayons; some are big on toy cars and
playing ball. I remember doing a lot of dancing with my little
ballerina when she was still in diapers. Working puzzles and
learning to count intrigue some two-year-olds, while others
are not nearly ready for such things yet. Two-year-olds do not
usually enjoy listening to mommy as she talks on the phone to
someone else or staying off the ladder while daddy paints the
house.

A good help in mothering a two-year-old is visiting another home with children. Playing in parks and such sports as
swimming and skating can be fun for parents and little children together. Parents who find it difficult to provide enough
interesting activity in their homes for busy little ones have
joined together to form play groups and play centers where
adults can go with their little children for fun and companionship. Other parents take jobs—paid or volunteer—at pre-
schools or day care centers so that the child can enjoy the
other children and the facilities with the security of having
mom or dad along. Parents also benefit from the companionship of other adults while caring for their children.

Of course becoming so involved away from home with
your youngster is quite an undertaking, and I do not want to
leave the impression that such elaborate steps are necessary

for all, or even the majority of children. Most children most of the time are quite adequately challenged by following mother around and manipulating ordinary household equipment. In fact, you usually do not need to plan your child's activities, but rather his environment.

Many of us worry about absent-minded mothering of young children, mothering in which we tend to our own business as best we can and just automatically nurse when the child comes for it. In fact, provided our surroundings are rich in people (like neighbors and relatives) and objects like pans, oatmeal boxes, hair-roller pincushions, paint and paper, and on and on through the list of "educational toys," absent-minded mothering, by which I really mean "non-manipulative" mothering, may be the best there is. "Good, wholesome neglect" Mary White calls it. Children learn much by being on the fringes of interesting adult activity, and mothers are happiest when we maintain some of our own interests.

The key to good "absent-minded" mothering is that we keep the environment changing (which really is not absent-minded at all, but rather sneaky and creative) and keep our own activities very flexible. What we choose to do must be easy to put down and take up again. Without great fuss you should be able to stop what you are doing (the secret is not ever planning to finish) and either nurse or go help with your child's project or just walk around and talk for a while. As long as you keep many and varied opportunities available, you can depend on your child to let you know what kind of attention he may need.

Non-manipulative mothers learn to listen to their children, to help them when they are bored and fussy, and not to interfere when they are busy.

Shyness, anywhere from moderate to extreme, is characteristic of some two-year-olds and can be a special challenge to parents. Many children this age are not yet ready to cope with all the people in a play group, or sometimes even visiting another home. When they are shy, children will often seek relief from too much contact with people by asking to nurse more often. These children need the same physical and mental exercise as do children who are more mature socially, but they need to do their work in an intimate family setting.

The swings and sandbox in the park down the street may be great fun for the little girl next door. But you may need to swing and play in the sand in your back yard or kitchen for a while yet until your little guy is ready to come out into the big world. He may not be ready to use that neat jumping horse or the huge set of blocks that the play group or preschool has, but you can have the same fun jumping off the porch with him or piling up your ever-increasing collection of cartons.

And allow me to repeat what I have said before: Your shy child will not necessarily be shy forever, and uneasiness in new situations is characteristic of most two-year-olds. The only way you can doom your child to a lifetime of shyness is to force her into situations that are too demanding for her immature capacity to deal with other people, and then to try to force her to cope beyond her capabilities.

There are times, of course, when you expect an increase in your child's need for nursing—during illness, when you move, when a parent or sibling is away more than usual, during busy times like holidays, and so on—any time that your child finds stressful.

Sometimes situations arise in which mother and child must be separated for some reason or when the little one must be around more people than he can handle comfortably. A little bit of stress from these situations or others will not all by themselves damage your child's progress in growing up with a healthy psyche. It is being forced to live with stress over too long a time and without plenty of comfort and security that will cripple her.

You can be observant and supportive in whatever way is available to you. If your child chooses to cope with stress by nursing frequently, wonderful! Nursing is certainly a convenient, wholesome way to help a little guy grow past a rough spot. If nursing is not available, then a bright and attentive parent will follow the child's cues and find other ways to provide comfort and security in times that the child sees as tough ones.

If you have checked into every aspect of your two-year-old's life with you and can see little shortage of stimulation or security, and she is in good health and well nourished, yet she still wants to nurse "all the time," I'd suggest that you stop worrying. Some children take a long time to come to terms with this world and need to be babies longer than what some of us may label as the norm.

These nursing-all-the-time little people are, I know, very wearing on their mothers; they make me think of young robins, bigger than their mothers, but still fluttering and cheeping to be fed. The robin mothers, like us, get really frayed and worn out babying their big fledglings. But they seem to know better than to abandon their young before they are ready to make it on their own. You can be sure that, provided you keep the opportunities for growth and more interesting "big kid" activities open and attractive, your child like the young robin will move away from such frequent and urgent demands on you as soon as he can. Eating hamburgers and playing with other children is a lot more fun than nursing, so it will not be long before your child will choose the companionship of other children and his own place at the family table instead of your lap. And like the mother robin, you too will then have a chance to get your feathers all preened and into place again.

RESENTMENT AGAINST NURSING

Many of us mothers during the time that the little ones need so very much attention, including so very much nursing, find ourselves feeling manipulated, feeling that our entire lives are dominated by the needs of our children. Young children seem so unreasonable sometimes, refusing (unable, really, but that is not how we see it at our lowest times) to pay attention to our need to fix supper or wash our hair or perhaps just to be alone for a little while. One mother of a two-year-old pinpointed what is probably the greatest difficulty we have as we learn to be mothers when she said, "I'm feeling that the baby is too dependent on me." Another mother complained, "Every time I sat down, there she'd be. I felt like a mother dog with a litter of puppies just waiting for mamma's knees to buckle so they could latch on."

No doubt the mother dog, who sees no option to natural mothering in her own canine fashion, and who is certainly not considering resorting to bottles or pacifiers to relieve her burdens with future puppies, still occasionally feels overwhelmed by her young ones' needs. Nor can she comfort herself by looking into the future toward a time when her life again will be more her own. Human mothers, though, have additional factors at work.

Few of us as we were growing up had any chance to observe and learn how people go about natural mothering, especially in the second and third years. The families around us usually had mothers who believed they must avoid as much as possible being personally and intimately available to young children. With no role models from our past to follow, we have the double task of, first, meeting the child's needs and our own, and also figuring out how. Caring for a two-year-old is a demanding enough path to travel all by itself; having to plan and clear our own trail as we go is what makes the second and third years so unusually difficult for us sometimes. Hopefully our daughters will find the way already cleared for them when they mother our grandchildren.

If we look carefully at our feelings about nursing, we will usually notice that we are not always overwhelmed by our children's needs—just part of the time. As I have said repeatedly, our worst times are likely to be when we have our priorities out of order. Yet there can be physical causes, too, at times, for our impatience with nursing. Right before a menstrual period many of us react against our children's nursing, and often in fact against any demands that are made on us. Nipple tenderness at the time of ovulation or pre-menstrually can add to any tendency to resent nursing. Most mothers feel a great deal of relief from any possible bad feelings pre-menstrually or mid-cycle just from recognizing the cause and knowing that they will feel better in a few days. Cutting down on salt and increasing fluids can also help relieve pre-menstrual irritability.

As we are learning to be mothers, especially the first time (though the truth is that we never stop learning), things do not always go smoothly, for we are still growing up ourselves. "Some days around suppertime both of us are uptight at the same time," one mother writes, "and I do not want to sit down and nurse him. Then there are the just plain *ugly* days, and I find myself screaming for nothing. I thank God on those days for being able to sit *us* down and nurse and love after mom gets it out—calms us both down." There is no way more reliable than nursing to help us and our children to get back to feeling good about each other after we have let feelings get out of hand.

Factors that make nursing difficult in the demanding years are not always entirely within us. Some children are just harder to care for than others. One mother described one of her children as "very demanding," "selfish," un-fazed by his mother's feelings. "He turned me off," his mother said; and this worried her. We can only wish these challenging little people were all fortunate enough to be born to mothers like the one who wrote me, mothers who resist their impulse to reject these children when they are at their worst, and who require themselves to remain open so that they can enjoy their children when they are at their best. Nursing is an especially valuable method of soothing the inevitable negative feelings that surface daily in some children—and in their mothers.

In the meantime resentment toward how much our little children need us is likely to be a part of the picture for most of us. It is nothing to be ashamed of, and we mothers can best alleviate it by sharing our feelings with each other.

CHAPTER 13

Nursing a
Three-Year-Old

BABYHOOD'S LAST SHADOW

Most nursing children at this time are weaned by their third birthdays. I have no doubt that many children wean spontaneously by this age in every culture. At the same time I am certain that the opinion held by most of our society, even those who are comfortable with prolonged nursing, that children this age should not be nursing, influences us toward weaning by three if not sooner. For this reason it is hard to say for certain whether three is a natural age for weaning for large numbers of children or whether three years is another cultural landmark, like age one. The truth no doubt is somewhere in between. There is no exact "natural" age at which babyhood and nursing must end. At the same time there are enough changes both in behavior and physical appearance in the fourth year for us to feel that babyhood fades out and childhood fades in sometime around three.

Every passing day in the life of your child does bring closer the day when weaning will be easy—maybe by age two and a half, maybe by age four and a half—somewhere along the way comes a time when you can wean without tears. At the same time, though, that the possibility of weaning becomes less overwhelming for your child, nursing usually becomes increasingly easy for mother. A three-year-old with whom you have been talking about nursing from infancy will usually go along with your nursing preferences and rules most of the time. Your growing child will rarely ask to nurse in embarrassing situations, nor should there be much problem any more with feeling that you have to nurse at times or in places in which you dislike nursing.

A three-year-old may not be ready to understand the complexities of your feelings about nursing (or about writing on the walls for that matter), but most are ready to live with a few reasonable limits based solely on your feelings. These limits may not make sense to him yet, of course. Your child has no built-in understanding of why you may prefer not to nurse, let us say at a concert in the park. Nor will she necessarily agree that your wallpaper looked better before she added her own finishing touches in crayon. But she is learning to do some give and take—to make some adjustments to living with you, just as you make adjustments to living with her.

As a result of the three-year-old's slowly increasing adaptability to cooperate, mothers usually find a nursing child this age to be a genuine pleasure most of the time. Nursing is almost always private, intimate, and enjoyable, often spiced with lively and profound conversation. Three-year-olds tend to be unusually pleasant people to have in the family anyway, so it is little wonder that, if nursing is still a part of a child's family interaction at this age, then nursing is unusually pleasant too.

The situations that work against nursing children in their fourth year are usually from sources other than just mother and the nursling. The most apparent events to lead a mother to decide against continuing the nursing relationship are pregnancy or the arrival of a younger sibling. A child does not automatically have to be weaned because of the younger child of course; but in many families mother cannot be comfortable, be it physically, emotionally, or both, with the child's continued nursing. So she initiates weaning.

Probably the most common reason for weaning a three-year-old is an overwhelming feeling on the part of one or both parents that more than three years is just too long for nursing to continue. Three-year-olds walk, talk, and are often pretty well out of diapers. They do not look like babies any more, nor do they act much like babies. And even those authors who are comfortable with extended nursing usually suggest that most three-year-olds should be pretty easy to wean.

Of course many of these kids still suck their thumbs, sleep with teddy bears, throw an occasional tantrum, or exhibit some other holdover of baby behavior. Fortunately for children and parents alike we are learning to worry less about eradicating these traces of infancy that remain in the intricacies of our children's seedling personalities. Like the seed leaves emerging in a young bean plant, your child will grow and spread himself until hardly a sign of his infantile form, with all its folds and shadows, remains. What we cannot predict, however, is exactly which babyish behavior, or "fold" will be the last to disappear.

It seems to me that if child-care experts advise patience, as they most certainly should, with somewhat disturbing infantile behaviors like thumbsucking and bedwetting in children over three, there is every reason that they should be even more understanding of such a healthy behavior as nursing. No one has demonstrated that any harm can come from continuing to nurse. Many families feel much good has come from it.

TALKING ABOUT NURSING—AND ABOUT WEANING

As children grow older and understand more about themselves and the rest of the world, most mothers want them to know that nursing is something they will outgrow and that mothers do not expect them to be nursing forever. When you mention the fact that he will wean sometime, though, a three-year-old who loves to nurse may seem incredulous. It is probably just as hard for him to believe that he will someday be happy without his loving closeness as it is for you to believe sometimes that he will not be nursing on the way home from the third grade play. The child who is not ready to grasp even the concept of weaning will usually ignore any attempts you make to start a conversation on the topic—or will pointedly change the subject. It is not usually so much that the topic is threatening; the topic is inconceivable and unreal to him, not worthy of discussion. If your child should feel threatened, though, he will probably respond by needing to nurse more for a day or two.

One three-year-old, his mother wrote, "would hear me

tell people that I'm going to let him wean himself. One day he said, 'Why do you want me to wean myself? I don't want to wean myself!' It took a little explaining to get him to understand what I meant.'' The idea of self-weaning did not make any more sense yet to this little guy than would have weaning of any kind.

When your child will not discuss weaning with you, forget it. Let it go for several weeks before you bother to bring it up again. By then she may have weaned quietly with never a word shared on the subject, or she may be ready to talk about the idea of weaning, or she may still turn down your offer for discussion.

The reasons for discussing nursing and weaning with your child are both serious and frivolous. One mother says, ''I think one of the very nice things about nursing an older child is that you can talk, and thus is added another dimension to the relationship.''

Some of their observations about nursing and weaning are jewels to ornament your life, and you should seek out such treasures without shame or hesitation. One three-year-old, for instance, schedules his day like a busy executive. ''Don't go away,'' he said, ''because I want to nurse when I finish this castle.'' When a father told his almost-three-year-old, ''Big boys don't need Mommy's milk,'' he replied, ''They sometimes do at bedtime!'' When a mother's let-down did not come quickly enough, one little fellow said impatiently, ''Turn it on, Mommy!'' And when a mother asked her little girl, ''Want to nurse now?'' her daughter exclaimed with delight, ''You have the bestest ideas!'' She may comment halfway through, ''This one all gone—other side,'' and after finishing conclude politely, ''All through. Please close door.''

On a more mundane level—back from the pearls to the brown tape and thumbtacks of living—mothers do not see nursing as quite the same sort of baby behavior as is needing a teddy bear or thumbsucking. On one hand nursing is less disturbing, because it does not carry with it so much the probability that some need or other for mothering has somehow gone unmet. On the other hand the teddy bear is a private matter for your child. Thumbsucking is also mostly his own business—unless you are looking ahead to orthodontists' bills should the thumbsucking continue into the school years. Nursing, though, involves two people, and mothers are not enthusiastic if they begin to feel irrationally that nursing might last as long as a few children continue thumbsucking or sleeping with cuddly toys. Some kids occasionally find themselves still needing these one-person comforts in their college dorms!

Once your child is able to handle the idea of weaning intellectually, for your own peace of mind you can let him know that weaning will occur, that you expect it to occur eventually, and that you will both still be loving and close even when he no longer needs to nurse. You can point out other children, especially older siblings who no longer nurse, not, let me make haste to say, as competitive examples. ("Look, Gwen doesn't nurse any more, and she's only two!") Rather, you should use children who no longer nurse only as examples to show that life without nursing can be secure and happy. ("Gwen used to like to nurse the way you do. She and her mother like reading stories better now, though. Someday we'll be that way too.") You are giving your child information which he will put to use in his own time—in a few weeks, or a few years, depending on his needs and his individual pattern for maturation.

For the fourth year is a time when the child's incredible early growth seems to reach fruition. It is for this reason that many who study child development do see this time as the end of babyhood. And children this age, even if they are not quite ready yet to leave behind all baby things, are usually eager to look ahead into childhood.

CHAPTER 14

Nursing Past Four

THE SPECTER OF NURSING FOREVER

Children who have not already weaned by four are almost always showing signs of weaning, or will show some readiness in the next few months. There is no way to know how long it may be before your child outgrows nursing altogether. Still, if you have been uneasily living with the thought that this child will not be able to go away to college because the telephone company has yet to devise a long-distance nursing system, you will feel reassured to see your child thinking about other ways to relate to you and other ways to feel loved and secure.

Unless you have nursed a child of four years or more, the idea no doubt seems horrifying—such a big child! Of course most of us felt that way about nursing two-year-olds when we first encountered them. If you are nursing a child in those particularly demanding second or third years, the idea of a nursing relationship that may continue past your child's fourth birthday may make you want to run away from home or something. You are right, of course, when the thought of mothering (not just nursing) this two-year-old for years on end seems exhausting. But just as all mothering changes between two and four, so does nursing.

These nursing children understand what you have to say

very well. Most children this age who are still nursing could be weaned much more easily than they could have been at two or three. At the same time, however, the reasons for weaning are no doubt all but gone. Nursing the preschooler who still needs this special kind of mothering is very enjoyable. They have learned not to embarrass you. They nurse with far less frequency or duration—or both. The nursing relationship with the over-fours with rare exception is little burden, if any, on mother.

It may become necessary to deal with an occasional suggestion that your child will still be nursing after he starts to go to school. "Why do you think they have recess?" many parents reply. And if the truth were known, we would soon learn that some fine people still enjoyed a bit of nursing when they were in the early grades and that there are well-adjusted school kids now who are not completely weaned.

One kindergartner used to ask coyly at bedtime, "Can I please N.U.R.S.E.?" Her mother writes, "I chuckled to think what some people would say if they knew a kid who could spell it was still nursing."

Yet, except for the secrecy that our social customs make desirable for those who are nursing past four, few mothers find any reason to quit forcefully. Nursing past four may become a bit of a problem as at other ages, because of outside factors such as pregnancy or fear that nursing so long is somehow bad. The nursing relationship all by itself is rarely a source of difficulty, but rather a pleasant cuddle.

BECOMING PART OF A MEMORY

Children begin to have conscious memories of their lives sometime past three or four for girls and usually a little later for boys, and nursing is one of the many things they may remember. You may be a bit frightened to think that your child, when he is grown and, say, an official in the Chicago City Government, may still remember nursing. Would sharing such intimate memories with your son or daughter in the years ahead embarrass you? Probably not.

The memories people have of nursing are full of the kind of tender warm fuzzy feelings which lead to institutions like Mother's Day. These were certainly the kind of feelings expressed by an actual Chicago City Official to a Convention of La Leche League International when he talked about his memories of nursing when he was little. What he had to say would not have made his mother uncomfortable; had she been there, no doubt she would have felt choked up and very much loved to hear what her grown son had to say. Nursing is a healthy relationship, and your child's memories of it will be healthy.

PEER PRESSURE

Long before your child reaches four you have no doubt worked out systems that protect you from receiving more comments or pressure from other adults than you can handle. Keeping older siblings from translating your "code word" for the uninitiated may be the only problem along this line that you yourself still encounter. As your child, however, gets older—maybe indeed before four, but certainly at this age—you will need to be aware of what is happening among her siblings or her friends. There will very likely be conversations about nursing—and there should be. There may also be teasing about nursing which you will need to monitor.

I would not suggest that you try to stop all teasing on this subject or any other among children the same age. To do so would be impossible, and probably not the best for their relationship if you could do it. Teasing is a significant part of childish interaction, and of human play even among adults. You do need to watch your nursing child, though, to see how he is coping with teasing about nursing.

Teasing of younger children by older ones can be somewhat different, because the opinions of the big kids carry more weight than those of the kids the same size. When a child, especially one who is three or four years older, is teasing a little one, we need to make an effort to teach him to limit his teasing to topics that are fun, and to a gentle enough level for fun. Older children need guidance on rules for the "teasing games" with little children, not only to protect their relationship with the young sibling or friend, but also as part of their education for becoming parents themselves.

If your nursing child begins to show signs of distress because of pressure or teasing from other children, you will need to do what you can to help him. He may show distress by more frequent nursing, aggression or withdrawal in his relationship with you or with the other children, increased problems with sleep, increase in bedwetting, thumbsucking, or any of the host of ways children tell us that something is not going right with them.

You can give your child relief by educating the children who are teasing about nursing so that it will not be such a hot topic for their verbal games. Also you and your nursling may decide on ways to keep nursing more private. A preschool child is certainly old enough to do some planning of his nursing times, particularly in his own defense.

Your little one will probably feel better just from having you bring up the topic of teasing if it is bothering him. Knowing that you are aware of the problem and want to help will take a lot of the pressure off all by itself.

Teasing on any topic, however, as I have said, is not to be eliminated even if it could be. Provided it is on a playful level and does not degenerate into ridicule, teasing is a valuable form of entertainment; people need lots of practice to be good at it, either on the giving or receiving end. Through teasing children learn some aspects of how to behave in a particular society. Many conventions of our life together are learned through teasing—learned not from adults who set up rules, but from other people at about the same time in life coping with pretty much the same things.

The role of adults in this process is the difficult one of keeping the "games" fair and relatively painless, for children do not know how far they can go on the topic of nursing or any other without hurting their companions. It is our job to teach them what is fair play and what is not. This part of our parenting job begins when our children begin interacting with other children and continues until they are grown. If the job sounds enormous, that is because it is. But it is worthwhile, for helping your children learn to tease fairly and enjoy being teased fairly is to provide them with entertainment for the rest of their lives.

The child who nurses to age four and beyond has an opportunity to apply her intellect to the kind of relationship she has with her mother and how this affects her interactions with her teasing peers and siblings. She comes face to face with inconsistent and contradictory feelings in herself, in her mother, and in other people around her. Observant parents

are usually aware of their children's working through the differing impulses of babyhood and childhood.

The nursing child is blessed with safe retreat when the
road out of infancy becomes too complex and uncertain. Some
growing children use nursing as a way to gain relief from the
emotional strain of setting their own paths through the confusion. Feeling relaxed and secure, they do a praiseworthy job
of coming to see and accept themselves both as individuals
and as members of society. Children who nurse past four are
not handicapped by their nursing as they keep growing.
Rather they capitalize on nursing as they come through their
"first adolescence" more smoothly than they might have been
able to in any other way.

PART IV

Weaning

CHAPTER 15

Natural Weaning

IN THE CHILD UNDER TWO

Because of the good results, both for their children and for themselves, parents are more and more comfortable with allowing nursing to take its course and waiting for weaning to occur naturally. Some people are choosing such an approach because it makes the most sense to them, as did the mother who writes, "She hasn't shown any signs of weaning, and I'm not going to push it. Why put a strain into a so far carefree experience? I believe it should end as it started—naturally." Others, like one mother of six, have more practical reasons. "She'll have to wean herself," she says. "I don't have the time to worry about it, and it doesn't matter." For these reasons and others, more and more children every year are fortunate enough to be born into families in which they do not have to give up nursing in anyone's time but their own.

A few children, of course, do come to a completely natural finish to their nursing before their second birthday. For the few who leave behind this part of their babyhood very early it will be in some other behavior that we will likely see signs of their immaturity for some time yet. Though they will continue to need babying, they will need it in other ways.

In this part of the twentieth century many more children than we might expect are weaning in their first or second year, even when there is no conscious effort on the parents' part to encourage weaning. One mother, disappointed when her fourteen-month-old weaned, says that weaning came from her approach to breastfeeding, not an active weaning campaign. She emphasized solids, offered other food before nursing once her child was eating solids, and did not nurse her child just for comfort. As this mother found out, children who start taking other foods and liquids before four to six months may come to depend upon these foods for most of their nourishment in the second half of their first year, a time when most nurslings still thrive for the most part on mother's milk. Often, though not always, children who take in a great deal of food and liquid other than mother's milk at six or twelve months tend to lose interest in nursing sooner than they might have otherwise. Often they will wean from the breast and cling to other comforters for months or years.

Some children have a tendency to lose interest in nursing to some degree and to become easily distracted some time between nine and fourteen months of age. You will probably find it easier to care for your child if she continues nursing, so do not hesitate to remind her to nurse a few times daily until she outgrows this possible ebb in her desire for nursing. The most common advice that you as a parent hear is that you should take advantage of your child's decrease in interest, if in fact her interest does show a decrease around this time, to initiate weaning. If you do not want to wean, however, the time around nine months, a little later sometimes, may be a sort of danger time in which you may want to make sure your nursing relationship is not interrupted or disturbed. Most children nurse without a pause through this time, and a very few will wean in spite of efforts to the contrary, yet you can nearly eliminate the possibility that your child might wean prematurely just by being aware of the time at the end of the first year and making sure to sustain his interest during those months.

Most youngsters around their first birthday still enjoy receiving a nice tummy full of milk when they nurse, and if we replace nursing too early with other forms of feeding and sucking, there will be, as a direct result, less of the milk that so many of these children look for. Besides, if we have bottles and pacifiers handy to offer our children, we ourselves are ever so likely to make use of them to put off a feeding while we finish this or that we are working on—which is one effective way to encourage weaning, whether that is what we have in mind or not. For many of these children such a pattern constitutes a satisfactory parent-initiated weaning. It is not a weaning, however, that is completely natural.

The way to achieve a natural weaning if that is your objective is to feed and care for your infant without contrived interferences. Nurse on demand from birth. Forget about other foods until your child asks for them. Then feed your child sensibly, for eating foods other than your milk in the first year usually is more for fun than for nourishment. Except in very hot weather a baby who has begun to ask for other foods does not need, besides your milk, any more liquids than he mooches from your cup or glass. An excellent way to avoid overfeeding or over-watering your baby is to let her do it herself, in her own way, and in her own time.

Unless you meet an unusual situation such as a tiny baby who is uncomfortable from getting too much milk at your breast, a pacifier is no help to you or to your baby. It is mostly a nuisance that, unlike your breast, is always getting dirty or lost. There is no need for bottles, either. Both pacifiers and bottles tend to become mother substitutes and are not satisfactory replacements for the full embrace of nursing.

Without the distraction and confusion brought on by pacifiers, bottles, and too much other food too soon, your child can nurse and wean in his own time and have a chance to outgrow his baby needs so completely that he can leave them behind, whether that be in his second year, or fourth, or whenever.

BETWEEN TWO AND FOUR

By far the most common time for natural weaning to occur is between two and four, with a significant number of Early Annas and Long Lingerers on either side of that age range. Weaning may come dramatically enough that your child will brag about it as one little girl did, telling her grandmother, "I'm going to be a big sister when I'm almost four—and now I'm weaned!" Or it may be so gradual that no one will know for sure when it happened.

For most children in this age range weaning is a gradual, unpatterned change in behavior, so unpatterned that it is not always even headed in the same direction. At times, maybe even for long periods, your child will nurse frequently and intensely. When conditions change, either around your child or as a result of his own growth, he will begin to prefer other things over nursing—playing, eating, sleeping, or even cuddling with you sometimes. Then things may change again for him so that he needs to be at your breast almost as often as before.

As the weeks go on, though, there will be movement, whether you notice it or not, away from many periods of frequent nursing toward more periods of less nursing. In some children this movement is regular and swift. In others it is so erratic and unpredictable that it is easy to understand how people come to believe some children would never wean without urging. It is quite common, too, for children to wean from one breast long before the other.

Such is the unpredictable course of natural weaning. At some age, very young, or "shockingly old," your child will not find nursing so absolutely essential to her well-being. She may stop asking so often. Or she may be distracted sometimes from nursing by anything and everything. You can see that, though she may have some months to go yet, she is on her way toward a time when she will no longer need you in this exact way.

You will probably respond, and appropriately so, to your child's increasing distractability as he matures. He may pull you to your favorite nursing spot, sit you down, latch on, and then instantly abandon you to chase his sister or watch a TV commercial. When this has happened several times, you will very naturally and with hardly a thought respond a little less quickly to his requests to nurse, at least when he seems to be asking rather superficially, and when the world around the two of you is busy and interesting. In this way, even without planning it, you begin to play your part in his weaning.

You will probably come to a time when you yourself are impatient with nursing. If you have been enjoying loving your child this way, you may be puzzled at the change in your feelings. No doubt your impatience will flare at times and subside at others, depending upon what is going on in the rest of your life. Some of what you may be feeling, though, is part of natural weaning and an indication that you too are gradually outgrowing the relationship. If you do find yourself less eager to nurse as time goes on for no reason that you can identify, there is no need to worry or to force any drastic changes into your life with your child. You too are growing toward being ready when the time for weaning comes.

In time—how much time no one can say—your child will abandon all but a very few favorite nursing times—usually when he is falling asleep or first waking up in the morning. When you are down to these few times, your milk production will probably dwindle. Then some children who have especially liked the milk will quit nursing in favor of breakfast or a bedtime snack. Others continue to enjoy one or more of these special nursing times for a long time yet, dropping them ever so slowly until a few days, then a few weeks go by with no request to nurse.

Once in a while someone suggests that your milk may become "poison" or "spoiled" if your child does not nurse for some certain amount of time. This is an old wives' tale; milk does not spoil in your breasts any more than blood spoils in your veins. Your child can nurse safely after any interval.

Not all children give up nursing gradually, though most do. Some children seem to reach a new plateau in maturity all at once and turn their backs on this or that baby behavior seemingly overnight. For example, one mother writes of her two-year-old, "He had always nursed to sleep, but one afternoon he got two new trucks and was afraid his brother would take them while he was asleep. When I sat down to nurse him he pushed me away, took a truck in each hand, and plopped down on the bed. He never nursed to sleep after that, though he did not wean from other nursings for several months."

It is very common for little people to toilet train themselves all at once. A few children also wean this way, especially when they are not nursing very often anyway. Surprisingly, the events that can bring on weaning in a child who is ready may be the same ones that may cause an increase in nursing at an earlier stage. A new baby, a move to a new home, or lots of company, often threatening to very little people, may at times be so exciting and pleasant to your older child that he will drop nursing to have more time to devote to the happy new circumstances. If your child is weaning quickly just because that is her way of doing things, and if your breasts do not become overfull, then let the matter rest and go on to other ways of being with your child.

Every natural weaning is unique, so that it is impossible to guarantee anything about it except that it will happen.

RESUMPTION OF NURSING AFTER WEANING

For most children before age three or so, weaning, natural or mother-initiated, is all but final when two or three weeks have passed without your child's tugging your blouse. After this amount of time most of these little ones do not ask again, or if they do, they find they have forgotten how to suckle. "Is it broken?" one little guy asked when he could not remember after a year just how to go about nursing.

Occasionally a child will ask to nurse again after you have regarded her as totally weaned. The most likely circumstance for such a request is when you have a new baby, but also once in a while when a child discovers that mom is pregnant. Or your child may be upset about something, or you may be able to discover no reason other than the mysterious workings of her growing little mind.

There is no reason not to allow your child to try nursing again, even though you have probably told all the relatives he is weaned. Chances are that he is weaned. A request to nurse from a child who has not nursed for a while, especially if the weaning was his own idea, is usually a request for reassurance and acceptance. It feels good to a little child to know that if he ever did need you again that way, that you would be there for him with open arms. One mother says of her weaned twins that they both had to try nursing several times when the new baby came, but gave it up after a few tries. It is much easier for a little person to wean himself if he knows that his decision does not have to be absolute and final.

One mother had nothing but positive feelings when her child wanted to nurse again a few times after over a year without asking for the breast: "I never realized just how important and memorable those nursing days were to her and that she would actually remember at all. This was her 'Thank you' for the loving patience and time I took when it was needed." A brief return to the mostly outgrown way of loving can be a chance for mother and little one together to enjoy a bit of reminiscing.

Once in a while a child who is apparently weaned will actually resume nursing for a while, most likely along with a new sibling, but sometimes for no reason that we can perceive. Such a change in events can cause you to panic, especially if you are very happy for your child to relate to you in a different way. Yet it will be helpful to your child for you to go along with him if you can. Just as we adults sometimes make a mistake in deciding to wean our children too soon, occasionally very small growing people make mistakes in deciding to wean themselves too soon. There is a reason, no doubt, whether we can see it with our adult eyes or not, that your child needs to nurse for a while again.

Though it may seem like it at first, you and your child are not going back to the beginning of the weaning process. After a few days of adjustment your child is not likely to nurse any more than do other children his age. He is not returning to babyhood, but picking back up a behavior that is appropriate for his age. He will nurse and wean also in a way appropriate to his age—maybe in the next few days, or maybe some months hence.

It will help us a great deal near the end of our nursing relationship if we realize that weaning need not be any more dramatic and final than toilet training. We are not surprised when a child who is supposedly toilet trained forgets and "backslides" for a while. It should be no more disconcerting that a weaned child would remember and "backslide" when he needs to. Especially in a household with a new baby, it can be such a help in overcoming a child's feeling of displacement for him to be welcome at mother's breast if he feels the need. There is no harm done by stepping back to baby things for a while—probably considerable good in the long run.

NATURAL WEANING IN CHILDREN OVER FOUR

One reason that we commonly hear to explain why most younger children do not ask to nurse again after they are weaned is that they forget about nursing. This may be true, though I am not sure. It is certain, however, that children over four (or even over three sometimes) do not forget about nursing. As I have said, many of them will remember nursing as long as they live. So it should not be surprising that children over four are notorious for going about weaning in an irregular way. Many seem to give a lot of consideration to weaning. One little girl, asked when she would wean, was clearly applying thought to the question when she replied, "Oh, probably I will try when I'm five, 'cause you can't come to school—*can you*?!"

Children usually wean at a time that is easy and stable for them. From their behavior it is often evident that they are making quite a rational choice for people so young. Some children tell their parents, and it is easy to see from watching some others, that they are weaning because they themselves decided to do so. In other children the process that leads to weaning is not so readily apparent; but this is probably not because it is so much different for them, but because they are children who keep their own counsel about it.

In the months that follow a decision to wean (or at least what appears to be such a decision) many children encounter rough spots that cause them to reconsider. These times can worry you if you have regarded the child as weaned, just as you might worry if a younger child who had been long weaned resumed nursing. You have not lost all the progress you have made toward weaning, though. A child this age who goes weeks or months without nursing is definitely working on growing up. When she asks to nurse again after such a long time you can be sure that she has just come to a time in her life which she can handle better if she can still nurse a bit. Once she works her way past it, she will get back to the business of weaning.

Many mothers with children this age are quite hesitant to say that their children are weaned, even after months without nursing. So often it seems that the minute mother pronounces her child weaned, he needs to nurse again.

Needless to say, spontaneous weaning with older nurslings can be gradual indeed!

CHAPTER 16

Time-Honored
(or Time-Worn?)
Approaches to Weaning

INITIATING WEANING

The primary message in this book is that weaning is something you can forget about, and that you can forget about it in your own best interests and your child's. There is no specific situation in which to recommend weaning, because no one knows of a 100% reliable substitute for nursing, either nutritionally or emotionally. Nor does anyone have an approach to weaning that can be guaranteed to bring about weaning painlessly or in a certain amount of time.

There are many reasons that mothers feel a need to initiate weaning, by far the most common being a feeling of disapproval from other people or embarrassment when the child insists on nursing in public places. Other less common reasons include drugs being administered to the mother, persistent biting, frequent breast infections, uneasiness with continued nursing, worry that the child is not eating other foods, pregnancy, or even illness in mother or child. None of these factors (except perhaps a condition so severe in the mother that the use of one of the few drugs known to be really dangerous to the nursling cannot be avoided or delayed) would make weaning absolutely necessary. In fact, some items I have listed, such as illness, are usually seen as an indication that nursing should definitely continue, at least for now.

Every family is different, though, and every nursing relationship is different. What motivates one mother to nurse may so overwhelm another that weaning is very important to her. Nor does the decision to continue to nurse or to wean either way mark one mother or the other as superior. Each mother is coping in her own way with the problems which her family faces and is acting as best she can toward her family's well-being.

Still, weaning before a child is ready is a difficult practice and full of risks for the nursling and for the whole family. Some weaning methods that we still hear recommended from time to time are so harsh that they can traumatize the child and leave him handicapped in his ability to interact warmly with other people for the rest of his life. For this reason, any "quick and easy" way to wean should be eyed with great suspicion.

MOTHER'S WEEK OUT APPROACH
—OR WEANING BY ABANDONMENT

Ask for advice on how to wean, and the most likely response you will receive is incredulity that you would be nursing a child old enough that you would need to do more than give the baby a bottle and take dry-up shots (not desirable or effective on either count, but this is what people believe to be true these days). The most likely recommendation you would receive if you kept asking, especially among your parents' and grandparents' generation, is that you take a week-long vacation, leaving your child behind. When you return he will have forgotten all about nursing—or so they say.

Even today the practice of leaving the child in someone else's care, whether inadvertently, or by plan, is a common way in which mothers wean their children. Sadly, it is not uncommon for families to plan separations—vacations and such—in hopes that when mother returns the child will no longer want to nurse. Sometimes mothers are part of the planning of these separations, or it may be that other family members make the plans and coerce the mother into going along.

This approach to weaning has serious drawbacks. It is certainly not to be recommended casually. Separation from the child, for one thing, is most unpredictable as a plan to produce weaning without a struggle and tears. Though it is true that some children left behind will not ask to nurse when mother returns, other children will. There is just no guarantee that this terribly risky practice will result in weaning. Even if it does, the cost can be entirely too great.

We adults may refer to the time we are intentionally away from a child as "separation," but to the young child it is desertion. There is nothing which can explain a mother's absence to a child under three or so (give or take a year depending on the child). Each child can comprehend mother's absence for a certain amount of time—maybe five minutes for some, maybe all day for others, and for some older ones maybe even a weekend.

Once you are gone past your child's limit, she may begin to mourn for you as if you were dead. She will be frightened for herself, wondering how she can survive without you. She may be furious with you for leaving her unprotected. She will begin to reorder her world so that she can get along without you, and her new arrangement may be a bit bizarre since she is not really mature enough nor in a good mental state, considering her fear and anger, to undertake such a project. She may settle on unfortunate and inappropriate behaviors to compensate for her loss of you.

Considering these things, I could not recommend planning much of a separation from a dependent child, for the sake of weaning or anything else. A mother of a nineteen-month-old was able to see risk in a lengthy separation even before she was gone. She writes, "I planned on taking a trip for one week without him. (He was to stay home with his father.) I tried substituting things when he wanted to nurse: toys, dancing, a bottle (Ha!), books, reading, or carrying him in the backpack. His attention was sometimes diverted, but only temporarily. I felt terrible, and he was frustrated. I cancelled the trip, and I'm glad I did."

As this mother realized, leaving a little one for long can be to take a deliberate risk, hoping that your child is one of those who will be unscarred by having you tear yourself away from him suddenly. The greater his attachment to you, the greater the danger that he will suffer from your unexplainable absence.

So real is the danger of a lengthy separation from a small child that even in emergency situations parents are going to increasingly greater lengths to stay with their children. Groups like Children in Hospitals have sprung up around the U.S.A. to help parents seek the best possible care for children who have to spend time in hospitals, including around-the-clock care-by-parent arrangements. These organizations also encourage hospitalized parents to seek visiting rights for their children.

Children are again on the scene more and more when families face crises or conflicts—while relatives bicker over an inheritance, at sickbeds and funerals, and so on. Nor do children suffer as much from being present on such occasions as they do from being shut out and left behind by their parents. Indeed children grow with a better understanding and acceptance of life and death if they are included as much as possible. Besides, little children can be a great comfort and joy to adults when events are trying or sad.

Separations do come up sometimes that we cannot figure out how to avoid. Of course a few years later somebody will come along with an idea that would have solved everything—that good old 20/20 hindsight—but the only thing that counts is what we can come up with at the time. When such separations occur, we must make the best of them and do everything we can to make them easier for the child—like keeping everything around her as familiar as possible. Once we are reunited, we must be aware of the strain that has been placed on our relationship. It is usually possible to smooth over the trauma of separation rather well with time and long-term availability to the child. One thing that will probably help is your child's ability to sense from your behavior that you grieved for her as she grieved for you. Homecoming would be a time, reason tells us, to make use of nursing as one tool for smoothing over fear and hurt feelings. This is a time to encourage nursing, not a time to try to stop it.

THE SPICY BURRITO METHOD

A technique commonly used to stop a child from thumbsucking has also, unfortunately, been used to bring about weaning. There is a foul-tasting liquid which makes thumb or breast quite unpleasant for the child. In some parts of the world mothers use something readily available in their own kitchens—a hot sauce such as taco sauce.

Like all quick-and-easy methods of weaning, this one carries with it considerable danger. The young child is actively learning how to trust dearly loved people. Though children must in time learn to be selective in their trust, they first must learn to have faith at all. Trust is a fragile characteristic that is rarely learned anywhere if not in mother's arms.

It seems too great a gamble to me to create even the possibility of shattering a child's trust in order to secure a quick weaning. We can only guess what passes through a child's mind when the sweetest and warmest part of his day suddenly becomes bitter, or even painful.

Of course it can be said that nature uses this very technique to bring about weaning when the mother is pregnant—at least this is what some youngsters tell us about the milk of a pregnant mother: It tastes bad. One three-and-a-half-year-old giggled, said the milk had turned to apple juice, and never nursed again. Others have less kind things to say about the milk of a pregnant mother.

In pregnancy, however, the milk must not become really awful, for so many children do continue to nurse. Nor is the change very sudden or contrived by mother (it would be very hard to keep a child in the dark about the source of the foul tasting stuff if we were rubbing it on). A pregnant mother is not deliberately making the milk taste bad. It is a natural change and an aspect of a real and natural condition. Children cope very well with real situations—it is the deceit behind a contrived situation that makes it so threatening.

Even so, some children who wean suddenly because of changes in the taste of the milk in pregnancy do react as if they have been weaned by the "spicy burrito" method and need extra attention and care for a while.

THE RETURN OF FRANKENSTEIN'S MONSTER

A variation on the bitter ointment approach used in some places might be to do as Gussie's mother did in *A Tree Grows in Brooklyn*. (This tale begins in the Introduction.)

> The neighbors found out about Gussie and discussed his
> pathological state in hushed whispers. Gussie's father got

so that he wouldn't sleep with his wife; he said that she bred monsters. The poor woman figured and figured on a way to wean Gussie. He was too big to nurse, she decided. He was going on four. She was afraid his second teeth wouldn't come in straight.

One day she took a can of stove blackening and the brush and closed herself in the bathroom where she copiously blackened her left breast with the stove polish. With a lipstick she drew a wide ugly mouth with frightening teeth in the vicinity of the nipple. She buttoned her dress and went into the kitchen and sat in her nursing rocker near the window. When Gussie saw her, he threw the dice, with which he had been playing, under the washtubs and trotted over for feeding. He crossed his feet, planted his elbow on her knee and waited.

"Gussie want tiddy?" asked his mother wheedlingly.

"Yup!"

"All right. Gussie's gonna get nice tiddy."

Suddenly she ripped open her dress and thrust the horribly made-up breast into his face. Gussie was paralyzed with fright for a moment, then he ran away screaming and hid under the bed where he stayed for twenty-four hours. He came out at last, trembling. He went back to drinking black coffee and shuddered every time his eyes went to his mother's bosom. Gussie was weaned.

The mother reported her success all over the neighborhood. It started a new fashion in weaning called, "Giving the baby the Gussie."

Considering some of our artistic skills, or lack thereof, I would think a child would be as likely to burst out laughing as to be scared of a face painted on the breast. But if the face should do its work and succeed in terrifying the child as in the story, then what would we have done? Everything I have said about trust before seems worth double consideration.

For a mother herself to create such fright in her child (not just a "boo" around the doorpost, but enough of a fright to cause weaning) seems terribly dangerous. The well-being of a child's psyche, the validation of a child's faith in those who are supposed to provide love and protection, is too precious to endanger it through such tactics as a monster where he has come to expect love.

CRYING IT OUT

Ever so many parents have been urged to ignore their children's cries when "the time" comes for weaning. There can perhaps be no more convincing example of crying that is solely for the purpose of manipulating adults, some people think, than a child crying for the breast. If your child's crying is for the purpose of controlling you, though, you should be able to perceive that in his behavior and distract him to a more interesting purpose, like controlling the dog maybe. Rarely is manipulation what an observant parent sees at all.

Instead, if your child cries to nurse, you are more likely to hear the need your child communicates in her cry. You will sense her pain if you deliberately deny her. Of course we cannot always give our children just what they are crying for, but still we do not ignore their cries. For you yourself will likely be miserable any time you let her cry and force yourself not to respond. Crying is a language for expressing human need, and we cannot hear it without being affected deeply.

By "crying it out" I do not mean to encourage you to fret every time your child cries because you will not buy him candy at the gas station or let him hurt the cat. Situations like that come up almost daily with all our children, whether we are trying to wean them or not. "Crying it out" refers to the practice of just letting the child cry rather than doing what you can think of to comfort or distract him.

To ignore a child's cry teaches him a lesson, of course. It teaches a child that even when he is so small and miserable that he can figure out nothing to do about the way he feels besides cry, still no one will help him. And as ugly as this lesson is during the day, it is much worse at night, the very time crying it out is most often recommended. For the night's fears can combine themselves with the loss of his mother's comfort to turn into the kind of nightmare we see in horror films.

Crying it out is just too painful both for parents and for the child and too likely to leave a scar of mistrust on their relationship. There is too much to be lost in flatly denying a child's expressions of need for a conscientious parent to do so for the sake of weaning or anything else.

CHAPTER 17

Some Less Dramatic Weaning Techniques

SERIOUS BUSINESS

The methods for weaning that have been discussed so far are intended to bring about an immediate weaning, a sudden weaning that is potentially hazardous both to mother and to child. Moreover, the advice of those who advocate such weanings usually carries a mild, perhaps, but still sadistic attitude toward the child or perhaps toward the intimate mother-child relationship. Such advice is often, if not always, based on lack of respect for the intelligence and potential of the growing child.

Weaning is a serious business in which mother and child can both be hurt by a bungled job. (I said hurt, by which I do not necessarily mean ruined for life.) Weaning is not some kind of joke to be played on a child or foisted upon a mother. If weaning is to be undertaken before either of the nursing couple is ready, then the people dearest to them need to be ready, not with derision, but with extra love and support.

Parents need to be on hand to help the child being weaned if the going gets rough. Family and friends need to be ready to support the mother if she is giving up the intimacy of nursing before she is ready. Just as we offer care to someone whose appendix is cut out, so we should be ready to help a person, big or little, whose nursing relationship is cut off prematurely.

175

Weaning is also hard work. Mothers who have actively weaned little ones who were nursing more than two or three times a day talk about a time of being very involved in the weaning process, with little energy left for other things. A common remark about the weaning time is, "I didn't sit or lie down in the presence of my child for the duration."

"DON'T OFFER, DON'T REFUSE"

After the publication of the 1963 edition of La Leche League's manual on breastfeeding and mothering, the weaning of choice in more and more families became the one recommended in that edition of THE WOMANLY ART OF BREASTFEEDING.

This manual encourages mothers to nurse whenever the child asks, but not to offer to nurse when the child does not ask. As the child becomes increasingly occupied with other things, the number of nursings gradually decreases until nursing stops altogether.

Don't-Offer-Don't-Refuse is a safe and effective weaning technique as families all over the world who have used it can tell you. It does not come with a guarantee, however, of how long weaning will take; it may take months or years. Once you have seriously undertaken the don't-offer-don't-refuse course, though, you can be honest in telling anyone who asks that you are weaning your child.

We should be clear in thinking about not offering to nurse and remember that this is a plan for weaning, not a directive for how to go about nursing.

Because the intent of this approach as presented in the original manual was sometimes misunderstood, being read to mean that a mother must never offer to nurse or the child will never wean, the wording has been changed in the 1981 revision of THE WOMANLY ART OF BREASTFEEDING. After all, it would be a shame, if you are happy to go on with nursing and let weaning come in its own time, for you to feel constrained against offering to nurse whenever you feel that is the best thing to do. There are times when, if you do not need to hasten weaning, the best thing to do is to offer to nurse—when you sense a tantrum coming on for instance.

At some point in the nursing relationship, though, particularly if it is a long one, you will probably without thinking about it find yourself waiting most of the time for your child to ask for nursing. As the child grows older most mothers just seem to make the change to "don't-offer-don't-refuse" automatically, even if they have never read THE WOMANLY ART, which is what La Leche League's founders were talking about all along.

It may seem surprising to some people that children do indeed quit nursing even while mother continues to offer at times, but they do quit. In fact, mothers are occasionally quite disappointed that nursing ceases before they themselves are ready. These mothers will tell you how flatly a toddler or young child can turn down an offer to nurse once he has decided to wean. As one mother puts it, "Remember if a baby wants to nurse she will, but you can't force a baby to nurse. If you try to force, you are subject to getting bitten—not hard, but enough to get the point across!" There is no way I know of to get a baby or child to nurse when he does not want to.

It is fine, then, to offer to nurse. You should use some judgment about when and why you offer, but at the same time, do not fret and try to analyze every instance. Your feelings about your child and your relationship should influence what you do more than what you reason or read about what you are "supposed" to do.

DISTRACTION

All of us use distraction to help steer our children past soft drink machines, or to halt a squabble over a toy, or even to avoid an occasional nursing. With some children this approach can be used to encourage weaning.

To wean by distraction involves considerable change in your pattern of living from day to day. It is necessary to avoid old familiar nursing situations and create new surroundings that your child likes. For one child this may include a great increase in outings to places she finds interesting, and lots of company and excitement. For another child this will mean quieting life down a lot to minimize situations that he finds threatening.

Mother must be like a magician, ready with her bag of tricks whenever she does not want to nurse. It is necessary to

That's for my milkie.

anticipate the request to nurse and offer the distraction before the child thinks of nursing. If you should chance to appear in the nude before a child you are trying to wean, for instance, you have probably eliminated your possibilities for distraction this time. Once a child has asked to nurse, distraction becomes difficult—often impossible.

One universal tool in mother's magic kit for weaning is to walk, carrying the child, talking or singing. Mothers who have weaned by distraction start to look exhausted all over again as they tell about their weary feet and aching backs from pacing the floor carrying their youngsters, or standing at night, rocking from side to side. They have, though, the satisfaction of knowing they were able to do something to ease their children's distress during the process of a hastened weaning.

A change in routine may be distracting, too, like sitting up instead of lying down while helping your child go to sleep, or staying away from the old nursing places. Other possible distractions include reading stories, singing, new toys (even a special "distraction toy") or new ways of playing with old toys, outings, bike rides, cuddles and tickles, visits from other children, and other fun things. Fathers are the best distractions for many children.

By far the most effective distraction for many little ones is lots of attention from parents, "doubling up on the time spent with the child in activities other than being at the breast," a mother of a one-year-old writes. Such attentions can even be rather elaborate, as one mother describes: "I would get out a little table of his about thirty minutes before a time when he often asked to nurse. We would sit on the floor next to the table and share a snack (slivers of liver were a favorite) and a drink. I vowed to give total attention to him for that fifteen or twenty minutes. I wouldn't even allow myself to think of what I was going to do after that. It worked: He didn't ask to nurse for a couple of hours unless naptime intervened."

Distractions of any type, including the very best ones which include lots of extra love, are limited in their effectiveness to what the child is mature enough to accept. Sometimes the distractions are more appealing than nursing; sometimes they are not. Only your child can tell you.

SUBSTITUTION

Most mothers who initiate weaning through distraction combine that method with the substitution of food for some nursings. Sometimes children, even those who nurse frequently, do ask to nurse because they are hungry. A mother who wants to wean can try to anticipate these times and offer an appropriate food.

Again, like any form of distraction, it is not very effective once the child has asked to nurse. Mothers who have used this technique like it best when it successfully satisfies a child who is wanting to nurse at a time when mother wants to be at work putting a meal on the table or some such. Mothers like it least when it means giving up that universally enjoyed early morning cuddle-and-nurse and instead getting up to cook an early breakfast.

Substituting food for nursing is a technique that should be used in moderation and with good judgment. It is not in your child's best interest to be continually coercing him to do what you want with bribes of food, especially sweet food like raisins. Nor is it in his best interest for you to bribe him except on

rare occasions (sure, we all do it now and then) with inappropriate edibles—like cookies or candy. When I talk about substituting food, I mean whole, natural foods that you are
happy to have your child eating. Your purpose is to forestall
his hunger so that he will not be asking to nurse for that reason, and you do not want to warp his appetite toward the
wrong kinds of foods in the process. Substituting food cannot
be used effectively to dissuade your child from nursing when
hunger is not what is motivating him.

Though you may for reasons of your own be trying to
hasten weaning, it is hard to know how long your child may
continue to have the need to suck; and of course such needs
should be satisfied one way or another. Many children who
are being weaned before they have outgrown this need begin
to suck their thumbs or fingers. On rare occasion a child will
turn to a pacifier. These behaviors are certainly second-best to
nursing, but can serve to provide some relief for your child if
her sucking needs are being frustrated by the weaning. It is
not wise to discourage such sucking directly. Instead it is necessary to redouble the tender loving care she receives so that
the use of the pacifier or thumbsucking serves only to provide
needed sucking, not act as a substitute for the mothering that
children must have.

Mothers who have nursed their babies are intensely
aware of the richness of the mother-child interaction when
nursing. Nursing satisfies so much more than the child's need
for milk or need to suck. So when they see their weaned or
weaning children needing to suck—thumb, pacifier, whatever—they make an effort to hold the child then, while he is
sucking, and cuddle or rock and sing. Others, upon seeing
this behavior in their children, halt the weaning for a while. It
would be a shame after the good start these children get at the
breast for them to begin to transfer some of that wonderful
trust they have developed to an inanimate pacifier or bottle or
to withdraw it somewhat into themselves again.

POSTPONEMENT

One of the most effective long-term ways to hasten weaning is
to put off nursing for a while whenever your child can accept
the delay. Such an approach can be more flexible than

attempting to eliminate a certain "feeding." Many children nurse so irregularly that identifying a nursing time to be eliminated would be impossible.

Whenever we ask our children to wait a bit for a nursing, we are weaning a little bit. But, unlike the little delays we ask for almost every day, active weaning would involve consistently postponing nursing several times a day or night.

The tactics we use for delaying nursing are usually other approaches discussed in this chapter—distraction or substitution. Some verbal children will accept an agreement to wait for a while. You and your child will be comfortable with postponement only if he is ready to accept a wait, and only if you are able to come up with a suggestion that will keep him from being unhappy about waiting. Holding him at arm's length and saying "wait," as every one of us finds out at some time or another, just makes your child more determined to nurse than he probably was when he first asked.

Postponement, used creatively and with a close watch on the child's reactions, can contribute to active weaning. It is useful, of course, only for those nursings that can be delayed. Nursing for falling asleep and upon awakening are each parts of specific points in time and cannot be altered much by this approach. Postponement, however, can be a gentle way to urge a child on to other things, especially during the day. And it is an approach to weaning that is very easy to adapt to different kinds of days—hard days for your child when he needs more nursing, and easy ones in which he needs less.

Though there is no way to know how long it will take to wean a child using postponement, it can hasten weaning considerably. Often once nursing has dwindled to once a day or less, mothers who are eager to wean tell the child there is no milk. At some point many children will accept this, but by no means all. For those who are not moved by such a suggestion, weaning will come, but not quite yet.

SHORTENING THE NURSINGS

Quite a number of mothers have found it to be effective and relatively painless to nurse the child as often as he likes, but not to nurse as long. You can nurse for a little while and then use distraction or substitution. Like all efforts to alter nursing patterns, this one is comfortable for some children and not for others.

Sometimes shortening the nursing time seems to speed weaning, perhaps because it eliminates nursing for some children as a way to fill blank and boring times. Instead mother and child become involved in interesting diversions until slowly nursing is not needed at all.

For some mothers, finding it possible to shorten nursings removes any discomfort they felt with nursing. For frequently it is the very long times spent nursing that leave some of us feeling restless and resentful. There are ways of course to entertain ourselves during long nursings, but there is no harm in trying to persuade a child to nurse for a shorter period of time when he is able to make that change.

Older nurslings, in fact, will eventually agree to nurse "just a little bit" or to "get through soon" merely because you ask them—and because you remember to thank them warmly and politely when they comply with your wishes.

WEANING BY CONTRACT

Sometimes mothers say to their children, "After Christmas comes, let's not nurse any more. You'll have lots of new toys then, and we'll play with them instead," or "You're getting so big now. After your birthday comes I think you'll be ready for us to read a story at bedtime instead of nursing." Quite a number of children reduce the frequency of their nursing or quit altogether when mother tells them—usually not completely honestly—that they need to save the milk for the new baby. A few children will go along with a contract of one sort or another, though to be truthful most will ignore you if you propose that they quit nursing for any reason.

Some children agree to the contract, enjoying the fun of making plans, but back out when the agreed-upon time actually comes. Though children must in time learn to live up to agreements they may make, it seems to me that lessons about not breaking contracts should be taught over such matters as picking up scattered blocks or sharing chewing gum. Nursing is so important to the child who is not ready to wean that his feelings about that are likely to overshadow any possible understanding of the meaning of a promise.

One way to wean by contract is by bribery. Once in a while a child is willing to trade nursing for a new toy or pet—and lots of mother's attention to go along with the new interest. It takes considerable maturity and readiness to wean before a child can actually give up nursing comfortably for the sake of something else she wants very much, as in the case of the three-year-old who agreed to wean so her family could have a new baby. (Her mom was one of the few women who do not ovulate while they are still nursing even a little bit.)

Weaning by contract does work occasionally, but very likely this is with children who are nearly ready to wean on their own anyway.

FATHER AND WEANING

All of the approaches to weaning that have come up so far are fine for the light of day when you are awake and at your best. They can all be exhausting if a mother undertakes them seriously, however, all by herself. They are often near to impossible at night. Any father who is urging his wife to wean their child, especially a young toddler, needs to know what a difficult role he might have to play in the process. Just understanding how hard weaning can be will be enough to change the minds of most loving fathers.

Almost every parent-initiated weaning that I know of has involved a great deal of help from dad. A child who is immature enough to need to have dependency needs met through nursing still has very great needs in this department. Through nursing, mother and child have a relatively easy system for taking care of most of these needs.

When a mother is withdrawing through weaning, however, from what I have to call the best and easiest way of meeting the child's dependency needs, finding adequate substitutes is frequently more than she can do alone. It is sometimes possible for father to fill in part of the time and provide some of the close cuddling and affection that the child needs so much. And hopefully, if the weaning is to progress without great difficulty, the child will be far enough along in his social maturation to be able to transfer some of that affection formerly reserved for mother now to father. Of course it would be better for all concerned if this could happen in its own time and not be hastened.

Weaning at night is especially hard for mother to manage lovingly without help. In her arms, especially at night, the little one expects to nurse and cannot comprehend her unwillingness. Nor, as I have said before, are either mother or child likely to be particularly rational at night. Yawning mothers do not distract or substitute with much finesse, nor are sleepy little people very open to any ideas beyond their most basic needs. Fathers in these families have been the people who have made a comfortable, humane night weaning possible. They have walked, rocked, fed, and otherwise tended to their children at night for the duration of the weaning. Usually mother needs to stay out of sight while dad is tending to the little one. This way he is more likely to succeed in his efforts to keep weaning at night from becoming a grim nightmare for everyone.

Even during the day many little children do continue to expect closeness with mother to include nursing. Though a mother who is working on weaning may be redirecting the child with considerable success, she will be grateful when dad is able to provide the distraction for a while. The most common way for youngsters to be weaned from bedtime nursings, for example, is for dad to take over the task of helping little people get to sleep.

If the child is not ready for weaning, too much responsibility for weaning, especially night duty, can work quite a hardship on dad, even more so considering that most fathers still have to get up the next morning and spend the day at work. With this in mind, I would suggest that no one, particularly a father, should urge a parent-initiated weaning, especially of a child under two or so, except in the gravest of circumstances.

An additional role that a father would need to play during weaning is support for the mother as a mother. In some families this has meant an educated change in his own attitudes. If mother and/or child are clearly unhappy with the weaning, he can then be the one to encourage them to forget it for now. Or he can be sensitive to the feeling of loss many a mother has as her intimate physical relationship with the child changes. He may also need to support her if she faces criticism for her decisions regarding nursing or weaning. Women appreciate any of these kinds of support when they are appropriate. Without such love, she may find her job all but impossible.

SPOT WEANING

Often it fails to occur to us when nursing seems to be just too much for us that there is an alternative to total weaning. Usually it is not the whole nursing relationship that is difficult for us, but one or two specific nursing times. Or we may be bothered, not by nursing, but by having the nursing times last so long. In these circumstances we do not need to try to stop nursing altogether; we can try "spot weaning."

Spot weaning can mean an attempt to eliminate a certain nursing just as if we were beginning a total weaning. Or it may be more satisfactory to attempt to substitute a nursing at a different time. In the case of long nursings, we might try to persuade the child to do something besides nursing after a comfortable amount of time at the breast. Or we could try offering more frequent, shorter nursing times to see if that might be more satisfactory.

Readjusting nursing, or spot weaning as I have called it, is always experimental, and always subject to more change. A spot weaning may not be permanent either. Frequently children are comfortable with the restrictions for a while, then need to go back to the old routine. Then comes a time when partial weaning is okay again, and so on. I have not invented anything here, but rather have put a label on something we all do as our children grow so that we can continue to nurse without stress.

WEANING BY CAPITULATION

Not surprisingly many a family has hastened weaning by letting the pressure off. Children who are otherwise ready to wean may be made so insecure by the efforts to get them to stop nursing that they cannot stop. One mother writes that she had had it with her three-and-a-half-year-old's heavy nursing demands, though it was clear to her that he needed it. At last in desperation she tried stopping all her weaning efforts and told him he could nurse whenever he wanted, and she meant it. Right away he tested her by asking to nurse every time he thought of it. Then she says, "Two months after I decided to let him be and not worry about his all night binges and seemingly constant nursings during the day—he weaned! All by himself."

Capitulation, or letting the pressure off, does not always result in such a dramatic weaning. But it is one of the most often effective "cures" for frequent or almost constant nursing, especially in a child of two or older. Of all the possible approaches to weaning, although it assuredly will not produce weaning in a child who is not ready, capitulation is by all means the safest and happiest for your child.

CHAPTER 18

Making the Best of Nursing or Weaning

DECIDING TO WEAN

So often a mother will find herself feeling the need to wean and yet being torn between the improvement she expects to see in her life and the fear of any hurt her child may experience as a result of weaning. First of all she needs to evaluate her child's need for nursing as best she can and decide whether she can really provide adequate replacements for nursing in her child's life. She needs to look honestly at the work ahead of her if she does undertake weaning and to talk the questions and the decisions over with other family members who can help "mother" the child and support her during and after weaning.

If you are considering weaning, and thinking the whole process through has not led you to discard the idea, then proceed gently, but decisively. Eliminate nursings (by whatever techniques you feel will work best for you and your child) as slowly as possible—no faster than eliminating one nursing every week.

While you are doing this, keep the burden of the decision upon yourself. Do not try to shift part of the responsibility to your child by being indecisive or becoming flustered if your child is upset with what you are doing. Unless you have made the firm choice in your own mind to give weaning a try, the whole process is likely to be a useless and confused time for both of you. If you are going to make an adult decision like weaning for your child, you must act as the adult while weaning is underway. Your child is not equipped to comfort you and reassure you that this decision is okay. It must be the other way around. You must do what you can to comfort your child.

The kind of relationship you have with your child, along with all the intangible factors in your temperament and his, and of course his own rate of emotional growth are the determining factors in how nursing or weaning will proceed. Whether you are giving yourself lovingly to your child and are feeling warm, friendly, and cheerful is important in how well either nursing or weaning will go. If you are feeling guilty about weaning or about pushing weaning too hard, you will be angry with yourself and as a result probably will not be as loving with your child. He in turn may well become anxious and demand to nurse more. If you cannot be confident and comfortable about your decision to wean and continue to offer first-rate mothering during the process, then your child is likely to have difficulties with weaning.

If you find that you cannot keep your child happy most of the time while weaning, then you can, unless your reasons are urgent indeed, make another adult choice. Just as decisively you can forget the whole thing for a while, or at least reduce the rate at which you are proceeding. With weaning, like so many other decisions in life, there is no harm in trying, just as long as you are watchful and ready to give up an undertaking that is not going well.

KNOWING WHEN TO ABANDON WEANING

If you undertake weaning, it is usually very easy to identify an approach that will not do for your child or that is at too fast a pace. If you are trying to wean and your child becomes upset and cries and insists upon nursing beyond your ability to distract him or comfort him, it is not difficult to figure out what the problem is. You clearly need to slow down the rate of weaning, change your tactics to ones he finds more supportive, or wait a while to try weaning. There may even be pleasant indications, as with the little one who hugged mother's neck and said, "I give you sugar; now you give me ninny."

Other more subtle signals your child may give you, especially if you are very adroit at distraction and substitution, may show up as changes or regressions in behavior. Disfluency (stuttering), which is very common in young children, is not always a sign of stress, but it certainly can be at times. You may notice an increase in night waking or an increase in clinginess during the day. He may develop an attachment to an object, like a bear or a blanket, when there has been none before. There may be a new or increased fear of separation from you. A very common response to weaning that is going too quickly is a marked increase in mouthing objects or fingers and in thumbsucking. Occasionally children who are being weaned too quickly begin biting people when they have never done so before.

Weaning may or may not be responsible, however, for the changes in behavior you may see in your child. Children are people—complex beings with a lot more going on than just nursing and weaning. And, whatever the cause, you may be able to provide your child with lots of extra attention, love, and encouragement when these behaviors occur and thereby see them disappear without ever knowing their cause. It is not difficult, however, to make sure that your child is not fussy or clingy or up so much at night because of weaning. Suspend the weaning for a while. Go back to nursing as much as your child wants, and see what happens. You may not see results immediately, though; it may take a few weeks for your child's anxieties to subside if he found weaning very disturbing.

KEEPING THE EFFORT WITHIN LIMITS

Another measure of whether weaning is going too fast is its effect upon you. The obvious problem that can come up from weaning too quickly is that your breasts may become overfull, making you uncomfortable or even ill.

You may also find yourself spending large portions of your day, or even of your night, working hard to keep your child happy without nursing. You can become exhausted and really resentful that weaning is taking so much from you. And your physical and emotional state will detract from your child's ability to cope with weaning.

When weaning is keeping you busy for more than an hour or two each day or night, it is certainly time to reevaluate your decision to wean. What do you hope to gain by weaning? Is weaning going to be worth what you are going to have to expend of yourself to bring it about now? What is the atmosphere in your home while all this is going on?

No one can figure these questions out for anyone else, of course. You alone, along with your husband, need to put limits on how much you will expend for the sake of weaning. Sometimes when we undertake weaning, we seem to feel that we are committed to get it done at all costs. This is not so. We can and should frequently give thought to what is going on so that we can determine whether we are progressing toward our goal at a comfortable rate or if weaning is just too big a project to undertake right now.

Weaning, as I have said, is indeed a serious business. Just as it should not be allowed to take too much from a child, neither should it take too much from parents.

WHEN WEANING WILL NOT WORK

It can be discouraging of course, when what you really want to do is wean, to see how much your child needs to nurse. If you are weary of nursing, the intensity of your little one's needs may seem staggering. Most of us come into parenthood unprepared for the amount of parenting young children need and for how long.

If your child is not ready, his behavior urges you to look again at why you feel the need to wean now. Usually with creativity, perhaps with encouragement and shared experiences with other nursing mothers, you can figure out how to be comfortable with nursing a bit longer. You can be reassured at least a little by the fact that nursing as you know it now will not stay the same forever. One mother says of her son's weaning once she had given up on leading the way, "I'm not sure whether he finally weaned because I quit pushing, or if it was a coincidence. I sometimes feel that nothing we did or omitted could change his inner timetable and that he weaned when he did simply because his time had come. On the other hand, he wasn't really free to do his own thing until I let the pressure off him."

Your child, like this one, will quit nursing whether or not you ever do anything about weaning. And should you still feel the need to wean after a few weeks you can always try again. The day is not far ahead of you when your child's needs can be satisfied in more mature ways.

Of course I do not urge any mother just to keep on nursing and hating it if that is what it seems to have come to in her life. Rather I would urge a mother whose child clearly tells her that he cannot give up nursing yet without being miserable, but who is unhappy herself, to work very hard toward making her own life happier. Nursing all by itself cannot make anyone unhappy. Unhappiness with nursing usually comes from frustration at being unable to meet certain expectations and goals—like being 100% socially acceptable or making all your own clothes the way you always have, or whatever—because of the unexpected demands on mother's time from the nursing child.

It seems much wiser, when a child indicates a need for much attention, and/or for much nursing, to take those ever so important needs as a given factor in our lives and to restructure our goals around what we must do to help our little ones grow up as well as they can. When a mother is unhappy, she should not just let things continue as they are. If she cannot see any way to improve her situation better than weaning, then I suppose she should give it a try.

Nursing, however, frequently will not be the factor that can change. Often changes will need to be in some other part of a mother's daily expectations. What is surprising is the improvement that comes once we set our minds to making a different change, one less traumatic to human lives—such as maybe leaving the beds unmade for a month or two to make time for an extra cup of tea during the day, or trading chores with dad so that he is the one who puts the little one to bed, or. . . . The lists of parents' brilliant adjustments are endless. The truth that these families learn almost always is that nursing is not the problem really, and weaning is not the only solution.

KEEPING OPEN ARMS

We all experience negative feelings about nursing from time to time. And we all on occasion turn away from our children when they ask to nurse, turn them down, tell them "no," or push them away. These are unpleasant moments that leave us feeling guilt and defensiveness all mixed up together. These are moments when we are not at our best.

Yet in the normal course of events our children are very well equipped to deal with these grumpy times that we all experience. Like the little monkeys in the introduction to this book they fuss and cling and struggle until they force us to do our job and take care of them. It works out.

It warrants re-emphasis, however, that problems arise when a mother begins to focus on nursing, begins to concentrate all her possible weariness and frustration there, and to push the child away almost every time he asks. This leads to a nasty struggle between them, with the mother feeling increasingly angry and the child feeling more and more rejected.

A mother may be looking so intently at nursing as the cause of the problems between her and her child that she cannot imagine receiving relief in any way besides weaning, especially if she is somewhat offended anyway by the idea of nursing a child as "old" as her little one is. Or she may feel so trapped in her resentment of nursing that the only first step she seems to be able to see toward resolving her feelings and needs is to attempt weaning.

Though each mother must do what she can to improve a genuinely unhappy relationship between mother and child, still, eliminating friction between mother and child by abandoning nursing seems rather like eliminating friction between husband and wife by abandoning sexual intercourse. In either case the problem cannot be in the healthy physical union between people, but in the feelings and attitudes they are bringing into their interaction.

Nursing all by itself cannot make you so unhappy that you set up a pattern of pushing your child away. Nursing is a behavior that nature very carefully reinforces with pleasurable interactions and sensations. And nursing children are made cute and delightful so that we want to greet them with open arms.

We begin to struggle with our nursing children because of other influences on our lives. Some, like pregnancy perhaps, we cannot alter. But many of the pressures on our lives that make it hard for us to enjoy our children we can change, or delay, or avoid.

Your child needs you to receive him with joy and enthusiasm most of the times he comes to you. For his sake and your own you must not let anything interfere with that acceptance between you. If you feel that you have to get away from nursing into a style of parenting that is more like what you may have grown up with, then give it a try.

If weaning seems to be the best course for you, then find the best way you can to go about it without rejecting your little one. It is essential that, as best you can, you and your husband and perhaps someone else who is dear to your child do as did the mother who wrote of weaning, "Nursing time was spent with her, enjoying other interests until she became too absorbed to notice the lack of nursing." The point is to move away from nursing if need be, but never to move away from loving.

Usually dealing with hard times in the relationship between mother and child brings us back to the business of testing our values and doing the best job we can of keeping first things first. Creative parenting, creative family living, learning to work for each other rather than only for the career or the house or whatever—these values and priorities will go far toward guaranteeing open arms for every family member.

WEANING IN AN EMERGENCY

In the very rare instance in which weaning is so urgent that parents cannot change their minds, they may have the unhappy task of helping a miserable child adjust to weaning before he is ready. It is best if a mother in this circumstance can stay with her child, comfort him, accept his anger, and be sure he knows that it is okay to be angry and that mother is angry at the situation, too. Clothing that makes your breasts inaccessible may help when mom cannot nurse. Parents can substitute, distract, walk, or do anything that helps the child feel better. Weaning should occur as slowly as the situation permits.

Such a weaning can be very difficult for everyone involved, and fortunately it is most uncommon that an unrelenting approach to weaning is necessary. Fortunately children who must be weaned will often sense or understand the necessity of a real emergency and will cooperate as much as they can, making the whole process easier for everyone. For that reason it is certainly wise to explain as well as possible to the child that weaning is necessary and why.

ABRUPT WEANING

Hopefully weaning should occur gradually, dropping a nursing time no more often than every week or so. There are instances, however, in which abrupt weaning is unavoidable, the most tragic being the death of the infant or young nursling. When this happens the mother is left full of grief, surrounded by people and by things which must be done, and with painfully full breasts. The nursing mother who loses her little one needs care and support as she adjusts to and comes to accept her loss. She also needs rest and instruction in how to care for herself so that she does not become ill in the process of drying up her milk.

For a mother who must dry up her milk, Gregory White, MD, of La Leche League International's Professional Advisory Board, recommends that she abstain from salt, not restrict fluids, support but not bind her breasts, and express only enough milk to relieve discomfort. If these measures are not sufficient to keep her relatively comfortable, she should contact a physician who is knowledgeable about lactation.

Sometimes an abrupt weaning is not so tragic. It seems that some youngsters have not read what all of us author-types have to say about weaning—that it should be gradual and all that. Some kids are nursing quite a bit one day and then decide the next day that they are weaned.

Frequently a cause—like a sore mouth from an injury, a sore throat, or a new tooth—can be identified for this sudden change in behavior. And, though we cannot always pinpoint the cause for sure, there probably is some problem from the child's viewpoint that motivates him. For this reason I would think it best to encourage a child who weans suddenly to go back to nursing, especially if he is two or younger. It is a shame to let nursing end on a sour note if you can help it. Some few older nurslings do wean abruptly in the natural course of life, though, and will have nothing more to do with nursing. When a child has made this decision, there is not much anyone else can or should do about it beyond making sure that he has ample opportunity to change his mind.

LIVING SHORT OF THE IDEAL

If you should come to the end of your nursing relationship with a weaning that you regard as less than ideal, relax. Join the crowd of us. I do not know any mother who has been 100% happy with the way she and her children arrived at weaning every time. We each must do our best with nursing and weaning—and everything else we do with our children. When we fall short (I do not say *if* we fall short . . .) of this or that ideal, we must shake off the thought of it—except perhaps for a resolve to come closer to our mark next time.

Parenting covers many years, and nursing and weaning are only part of the whole picture. If you do not fail to measure up to your standards on one of these, then you will fall short somewhere else. Parenting is a job in which we need to do our best day by day. That is what books like this are for—to help us do our best. But we must not get bogged down in concern over every moment in our lives with our children.

We are not putting our children's lives together by some immutable scientific formula. Rather we are weaving a tapestry along with our children, a tapestry made up of our triumphs and our "If-only-I-had . . ." moments. The odds are on our side that years from now when we are finished, the tapestry will be very beautiful, and that the memories we and our children have of their young years will be joyful.

EFFECTS OF WEANING ON MOTHER

Weaning marks a significant but hopefully not drastic change in the way you and your child interact with each other. Like any other such change there is a whole collection of feelings that tend to go along with it. The more gradual the weaning, the more diffuse and easy to handle your emotional responses are likely to be.

Most of us at one time or another during weaning experience a sense of loss—loss of the nursing relationship, maybe the loss of an early morning cuddle in bed, a funny kind of tug on your blouse, and the like. Some of us wonder for a while if we have lost our status as the irreplaceable caretaker for the child, though of course we have not. Many of us miss the larger breasts that go with nursing. (When you have been nursing your children one after the other for the past ten years or so, the possible decrease in breast size when the last one weans can be a surprise.)

We seldom think of ourselves as having an emotional need for nursing our babies, or if we think about it, we tend to believe that feeling this way must be a little bit unhealthy or unnatural. Nursing is a symbiotic relationship, though, not just in the first few months, but for as long as we are nursing our children. A long and happy beginning at the breast is priceless for the well-being of our children; it is also important to our growth and well-being as mothers. We, as well as our children, can be frustrated by a premature weaning.

In reading letters about nursing from hundreds of mothers, I became increasingly aware of mothers who were sad or had mixed feelings when weaning occurred—the ones who were "singing empty nest songs" as it were. So many mothers whose children were weaned before two or so seemed to feel some sense of loss as did the mother who, after her eighteen-month-old weaned, said, "At the time I was semi-depressed. . . . But soon I realized that weaning was not the end of things, but the beginning of a new growth and another 'time of wonder' for us."

When nursing continues past two or three, mothers much less frequently describe weaning in the same mixed terms. It seems that a time comes in the growth of the mother-child relationship when it is easier for both to move on and leave baby things behind.

Of course relating mothers' feelings about weaning to the age of the child at the time is a broad generalization. Mothers' feelings also vary a great deal according to how the weaning came about and according to the warmth and closeness of the mother-child relationship before, during, and after weaning. It may indeed be that some mothers who are sad following weaning feel this way because of something in the mother-child relationship that has not worked out well, something that may in fact have led to the weaning. This could be true at any age. But having said this, it still seems to me that most of the sadness upon weaning that mothers have shared with me resulted from the fact that weaning came about before these mothers' nursing urges were completely satisfied. The source of such frustration for mothers is not usually from a child who chooses to wean too quickly on his own, but can be found rather in customs and social restrictions that interfere with the normal course of nursing and mothering.

While acknowledging the sad feelings that may go with weaning, we must emphasize the good ones. It feels good to reclaim our bodies and enjoy again an increased sense of privacy. Also, children who wean spontaneously do so because they are older and are becoming less immature. So along with the possible loss of status as the only one who can care for and comfort the child, most of us enjoy the freedom of knowing he can now sometimes get along very nicely in the care of certain other loving people. (This is true because he is older, not because he is weaned, and is not likely to be as true of a child who is weaned before he is ready.)

One mother shares her pleasure in nursing and weaning quite eloquently when she says, "The entire nursing experience was a blessing that I can't find words to express properly. Weaning came about so naturally and mutually there were no feelings of loss or inadequacy . . . or anxiety. . . . To me child-led weaning is like a beautiful conclusion to a novel. I came away from the experience with a sense of completion and total satisfaction. The wonderful thing is that it isn't the end, but only the beginning of the childhood years of growing together."

There are joys as well as difficulties in every part of parenting. The nursing years are not the only, or even necessarily the best, of our lives with our children. Babies are delightful to have around. So are school kids and teenagers and grown children. Through all the times of our lives we need to stay physically close and not let weaning be the end of cuddling and loving. (You're never too old to kiss your mother, they say—or your father either.) Above all we must not lose the special joys of the present by spending too much time regretting the loss of a way of living we have outgrown.

The best way I know of not to find yourself singing those "empty nest" songs as your children grow is to throw yourself into every phase of your growth as a mother. Follow your maternal feelings with your babies and young children. Exercise your mothering urges; wear them out; use them up. These urges will not go away, of course, but, like your child, you can be satisfied and fulfilled. You can grow with your children so that your move from your nursing rocker to the Blue Birds or to being a grandmother is as exciting and joyful as your children's.

Weaning is a time when we all look back wistfully at those precious baby years. And we are likely to have a lump in our throats at times like that. But there is just too much good in living to use up very much of life trying to stay where we are. It is better to let a tear or two fall if need be, put an arm around that dear child, and plunge ahead into the rest of your life.

About the Author

Norma Jane Bumgarner is a native of Oklahoma. She attended public schools in Norman, Oklahoma, and graduated with a BA and MA in Latin from the University of Oklahoma. "It is only then," she says, "that I began my true career—being a mother."

Norma Jane and her husband, Bill, are busy with three sons and a daughter. Three of the four children nursed well past their first birthdays. Norma Jane says, "None of the children were weaned or toilet-trained, yet none of them nurse any more—or wear diapers either."

Much of the family's time in the past few years has been spent at Seth's basketball games, Carmen's dance recitals, Myles' football games, and especially at their soccer matches. All of the children, including Vincent, love playing soccer. In fact, Seth has recently abandoned basketball in favor of the black uniform of a soccer referee.

Norma Jane has been very active in La Leche League for fourteen years. For five years she served as Coordinator of Leaders for Oklahoma. At the time of this writing she is Regional Administrator of Leaders for Latin America and the West Indies.

A frequent contributor to La Leche League publications and speaker at LLLI conferences, she is also the author of *Helping Love Grow, Some Hints for Mothering Your Adopted Baby.*

BIBLIOGRAPHY

Becroft, T. C. Child-rearing practices in the Highlands of New Guinea: a longitudinal study of breastfeeding. *The Medical Journal of Australia.* 2:598–601, 1967.

Berg, A. *The Nutrition Factor.* Washington, D.C.: The Brookings Institute, 1973.

Bowlby, J. *Attachment.* New York: Basic Books, 1969.

Brazelton, T. B. Parenting in another culture. *Redbook,* May 1979, p. 94.

Cardozo, A. R. *Woman at Home.* Garden City, New York: Doubleday & Co., Inc., 1976.

Finch, C. A. Iron metabolism. *Nutrition Today,* Summer 1969.

Grief: a peril in infancy. New York University, 1947. Film.

Hymes, J. L. *The Child under Six.* Englewood Cliffs, New Jersey: Prentice-Hall, Inc., 1963.

———. Behavior and discipline. Speech presented at La Leche League International Conference, San Francisco, 1976.

Kippley, S. *Breastfeeding and Natural Child Spacing.* New York: Penguin Books, 1975.

La Leche League International, Inc. *The Womanly Art of Breastfeeding.* Franklin Park, Illinois, 1963, 1981.

La Leche League of New York State. Little nursing persons—an in-depth look. *New York State Blender,* Fall 1975.

McMillan, J. A. et al. Iron sufficiency in breast fed infants and the availability of iron from human milk. *Pediatrics* 58: 686–91, 1976.

Mead, M. and N. Newton. Cultural patterning of perinatal behavior. In *Childbearing: Its Social and Psychological Aspects.* S. A. Richardson and A. F. Guttmacher, eds. Baltimore: Williams and Wilkins, 1967.

202

Newton, N. *The Family Book of Child Care.* New York: Harper & Row, 1957.

———. Nursing the toddler. Speech presented at La Leche League International Conference, Chicago, 1971.

——— and M. Theotokatos. Breastfeeding during pregnancy in 503 women: does a psychobiological weaning mechanism in humans exist? *Proceedings of the Fifth International Congress of Psychosomatic Obstetrics and Gynecology.* L. Zichella, ed. London: Academic Press, 1980.

Pediatric News. Day-care center role in diarrhea seen. August 1979.

Robinson, C. H. *Normal and Therapeutic Nutrition.* New York: MacMillan Publishing, Inc., 1972.

Ryerson, A. J. Medical advice on child-rearing, 1550–1900. *Harvard Educational Review* 13: 302–323, 1961.

Salk, L. and R. Kramer. *How to Raise a Human Being.* New York: Random House, 1969.

Smith, B. *A Tree Grows in Brooklyn.* New York: Harper & Row, 1947.

Thevenin, T. *The Family Bed.* Minneapolis: Privately published, 1967.

van Lawick-Goodall, J. *In the Shadow of Man.* New York: Houghton Mifflin Co., 1971.

Zilberg, B. How my four-year-old haunted our midnight feedings. *Redbook,* February 1972, p. 30–2.

RESOURCES

For further information about all aspects of breastfeeding contact:
La Leche League International
9616 Minneapolis Avenue
Franklin Park, IL 60131, U.S.A.
(312) 455-7730

To find the nearest La Leche League Group, consult the white pages of your telephone directory or write to La Leche League International.

In Canada, write to:
LLLI Canadian Supply Depot
Box 70
Williamsburg, Ontario, Canada K0C 2H0

Many of the books referred to in this text are available from La Leche League International. Additional sources of books relating to breastfeeding and parenting are:
Birth and Life Bookstore, Inc.
P. O. Box 70625
Seattle, WA 98107, U.S.A.

International Childbirth Education Association
BookCenter
P. O. Box 20048
Minneapolis, MN 55420, U.S.A.